T0248089

THE LITTLE BOOK

OF TRADING OPTIONS LIKE THE PROS

Little Book Big Profits Series

In the Little Book series, the brightest icons in the financial world write on topics that range from tried-and-true investment strategies to tomorrow's new trends. Each book offers a unique perspective on investing, allowing the reader to pick and choose from the very best in investment advice today.

Books in the Little Book series include:

THE LITTLE BOOK

OF
TRADING OPTIONS
LIKE THE PROS

Learn How to Become the House

DAVID BERNS

MICHAEL GREEN

WILEY

Published by John Wiley & Sons, Inc., Hoboken, New Jersey.
Published simultaneously in Canada.

For general information on our other products and services or for technical support, please contact our Customer Care Department within the United States at (800) 762-2974, outside the United States at (317) 572-3993 or fax (317) 572-4002.

Wiley also publishes its books in a variety of electronic formats. Some content that appears in print may not be available in electronic formats. For more information about Wiley products, visit our web site at www.wiley.com.

Library of Congress Cataloging-in-Publication Data:

ISBN 9781394238958 (Cloth)
ISBN 9781394238965 (ePub)
ISBN 9781394238972 (ePDF)

Cover Design: Paul McCarthy

SKY10069149_031124

For my Carolee & Henry, who bring magic to us all.
—DB

To Jennifer, Ryan, Ella & Gavin.
The journey has been the reward.
—MG

Contents

Chapter Six

Preface

---∽---

Retail options trading has exploded in popularity over the past few years. But options are complex, and trading options can quickly become a black hole of losses. The goal of this book is to show new options traders how to quickly pivot from naïve strategies with a high probability of loss to a winning strategy deployed by professional options traders. After a quick review of the option ecosystem and the basics of options, we spend most of the book presenting a proven options trading strategy. This strategy is a bread-and-butter trade from the institutional world of hedge funds and market makers, and we show you how to execute it at home. We have also decided to support readers of this book beyond just the words found here, by making the option screener reviewed in this book available for free at www.tradingoptionslikethepros.com.

This book is intended for nonfinance professionals. We have avoided the use of advanced mathematics to keep this accessible for all. We have thrown in a few "Adult Swim" sections for those who want to go a bit deeper on topics, but these are not required reading, so feel free to skip these if you want to keep things light.

Let's now quickly review what will be covered in each chapter.

Chapter 1. Trading Options: Allure vs. Reality. We review the recent rise of retail options trading, which has boomed on the heels of easy access to trading and an expansive social media ecosystem for amateur traders. We then illustrate how the combined human biases of loss aversion and overestimation of low-probability events leads novice traders into buying cheap options. We then show that most cheap options expire worthless, leaving amateur traders destined to perform poorly. This discussion lays the groundwork for the winning option strategy we will cover in this book: selling cheap options for small yet consistent wins.

Chapter 2. The Barebones Option Primer. We begin with a review of the defining characteristics of an option: calls versus puts, the underlying asset, strike, and expiry. We review the basic payoff structure of an option as a function of the underlying price at contract expiry. We bring time into the equation, showing how the value of an option contract evolves into expiry, which then forces us to break down option prices into intrinsic and extrinsic value components. The last part of our primer shows readers how to create spreads, where we simultaneously buy and sell options. Finally, we walk readers through a series of real-world examples to help solidify the core knowledge needed for the remainder of the book.

Chapter 3. Become the House. In this chapter we shift focus from foundational understanding of options to strategic application, specifically emphasizing the advantages of selling options over buying them. The chapter begins with a review of the option ecosystem beyond the novice traders highlighted in Chapter 1, showcasing the demand from both amateur and professional investors for different types of options, and creating opportunities for option sellers in various market segments. We then explore the analogy of option sellers acting as "the house" in three different business models: a casino, an insurance company, and a bank. This analogy helps illustrate how selling options can be likened to these businesses, each with its own risk-and-reward profile.

The core of the chapter then introduces our primary strategy: selling equity put spreads. We delve into why this strategy is advantageous, backed by empirical data highlighting strong profitability, high win rates, and limited losses. The rationale behind the specific strike selection and the 2-week expiry period is explained in detail, balancing the goal of maximizing returns while minimizing risk and operational challenges. We conclude by showing real-world applications of the strategy through a series of examples and empirical data, setting the stage for more advanced concepts and strategies in subsequent chapters.

Chapter 4. Risk Management. We delve into enhancing our core SPY put spread selling strategy, focusing on optimizing risk management techniques. The chapter underscores the significance of implementing stop losses, emphasizing their role in substantially reducing mean losses without affecting overall returns. We recommend an at-the-money (ATM) stop loss for the specific SPY put spreads and introduce the concept of "rolling options down and out" following an ATM stop-loss trigger. This approach shifts probabilities in the trader's favor, with an optimal rolling period identified as being more than 10 days to expiry. The chapter balances the discussion of stop losses with the exploration of profit-taking strategies, examining their impact on the strategy's performance. Unlike stop losses, early profit-taking reduces aggregate returns and increases some risks.

Chapter 5. Portfolios of Option Trades. Up to this point, we have focused on a single trade, the 2-week OTM SPY put spread. In Chapter 5, we expand the conversation to additional underlying assets and consider call spreads. We create more robust trading strategies by trading a broader suite of options, diversifying the portfolios and lowering risk. We also show that option premiums fluctuate dramatically over time and that this can meaningfully affect the outcomes of your trading strategy. As a result, being prepared to sell across multiple underliers can help ensure more consistent income.

We then focus on our preferred approach to constructing a portfolio of option spreads. Our "commonsense" portfolio diversifies our core SPY trade into other assets with a low likelihood of simultaneous max loss. We consider more sophisticated optimization paradigms to help build intuition around how an optimizer works, but emphasize the risks of rigid rules due to rapidly evolving markets and their "in-sample" nature.

Chapter 6. From Theory to Practice. At this point you will have the theoretical and empirical knowledge you need to sell options intelligently. It is now time to learn how to implement these concepts in the real world, sending you off on what will hopefully be a fun and lucrative trading journey. The chapter begins with a review of a real-time trade selection process, the key tool for selecting precise spreads to sell in your portfolio. We then walk the reader through the entire trading workflow to ensure effective trade execution. We also describe what we believe the first six months of this new journey should look like: a measured ramping up of complexity and risk to ensure all the basics of the strategy are well baked before big dollars and complex trades are executed. Finally, we wrap up with a conversation about the biases you must be aware of as a strategist, including confirmation, recency, and overconfidence biases.

Acknowledgments

———— ∼ ————

First and foremost, thank you to our amazing families for supporting us while writing this book, and more broadly, as we keep pursuing our professional dreams. We'd also like to thank the entire team at Simplify Asset Management for giving us the opportunity to share some of our most important tools and insights with the broader options trading community, especially those new to the endeavor. We are especially grateful to Emilio Freire, who coded up all the strategies and tools discussed in the book, making our job writing a thousand times easier. We are also immensely thankful to John Downing, whose incredible insights on options trading have greatly shaped the ideas in this book. Additional thanks go to David Jackson, Larry Kim, Eric McArdle, Olga Huxoll, and Pat Hennessy for incredibly valuable feedback and assistance on the final manuscript. And finally, thank you to Bill Falloon and the rest of the Wiley team for their gracious support and encouragement all along the way.

Chapter One

Trading Options: Allure vs. Reality

IN THE PAST DECADE, the allure of options trading has captivated the imagination of millions of new investors. Stories of life-changing sums being made overnight have contributed to options trading's new reputation as a pathway to instant wealth, yet the reality is far less rosy. In this chapter we dismantle the romanticized image of options trading that has become popular and present a professional's view of what successful options trading looks like.

Key Takeaways:

1. Easy access to trading platforms and online trading communities has created a boom in retail options trading.
2. Amateur options traders favor buying cheap call options due to two natural human biases: aversion to extreme losses and overestimation of low-probability events.
3. These cheap options almost always expire worthless, creating a headwind that is difficult for even the most sophisticated investors to overcome.
4. The professionals' path to successful options trading is to sell options for small yet consistent profits.

The Retail Option Explosion

Opening a brokerage account in 1990 to trade options required a physical visit to a brokerage office. A well-dressed gentleman (they were almost always men) would hand you a paper application several pages in length, which you'd have to fill out by hand. This form would ask for personal identification information, financial details, investment experience, and your understanding of the risks associated with trading options.

Brokerages in 1990 would have been particularly stringent about ensuring that you understood the products you intended to trade. You might have taken a questionnaire required to demonstrate a certain level of knowledge about options, option strategies, the risks involved, and financial markets in general.

Given the risks associated with options trading, brokerages would have also required proof of your financial situation, including your net worth, liquid net worth, income, and investment objectives. They would assess this information to determine whether options trading was suitable for you and which level of options trading you'd be authorized to engage in.

After submitting your application, the approval process would likely have taken several days or even weeks. Unlike today's near-instant online approvals, a team at the brokerage firm would review your application. You had no guarantee of approval—or realistic appeal process if denied.

Even after approval, trading options in 1990 would have been a broker-assisted process. You'd place trades over the phone by speaking directly with a broker, who would execute the trades on your behalf. This process was not nearly as immediate as clicking a button on a trading platform. During times of high market volatility, it could be stressful and time-consuming. It was also expensive. Option commissions often included a base commission per trade of $30–50 (over $100 today if inflation-adjusted) and a "per contract" charge of $2. Total commission on a $100 trade could easily exceed $50, discouraging small traders from participating and encouraging the purchasing of longer-dated options.

But today, options trading access is entirely different. One can open an options trading account in minutes without net worth or investment experience requirements. Brokerage houses have pursued options traders aggressively, reducing commissions on options (in many cases to "free") and making margin accounts easier to open than ever.

Figure 1.1 from a recent study on the success of retail options traders (de Silva, So, and Smith, 2023) demonstrates the recent boom in retail options trading. This data only covers Nasdaq exchanges (it turns out to be quite tough to access options trading data that discerns retail traders explicitly), but this should nicely represent the boom in retail trading seen across all options exchanges.

Social media has also played a massive role in this retail option boom, as anyone with an internet connection can claim to be an options trading guru. Online platforms are awash with individuals showcasing astronomical trading profits, complete with screenshots of their six-figure accounts. However, it's crucial to remember that these snapshots do not indicate consistent success but are often the result of high-risk strategies that could just as easily have led to catastrophic losses.

Figure 1.1   Retail Options Trading Volume on Nasdaq Options Market and Nasdaq PHLX

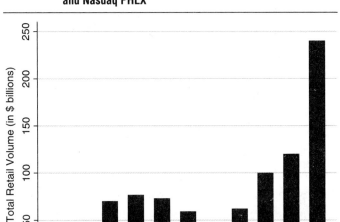

A shining example of the impact of social media was the meme stock craze between 2020 and 2021. "Meme stocks" refers to stocks that gained rapid popularity through social media platforms and forums like Reddit, particularly the subreddit r/wallstreetbets. GameStop (GME) and AMC Entertainment (AMC) were prime examples of such stocks.

Hedge funds and other institutional investors had heavily shorted many of these stocks due to poor fundamentals. Shorting stock involves borrowing shares from other investors and selling them with the hope of buying them back at lower prices in the future. If a company's stock has been heavily shorted, it means that finding shares to borrow or buy can be challenging. Recognizing that collective action could create "short squeezes" that would require these investors to rush to buy back their positions due to risk limits, groups of retail investors, with the aid of social media platforms, gathered to go long these stocks and force a squeeze of the institutional shorts.

Other retail traders, bored in their homes and sitting on COVID-19 pandemic stimulus checks, came out en masse. These new investors focused on options due to their lower cost of entry and limited (or "capped") loss potential compared to buying stocks outright. The options could also provide significant leverage, as traders can effectively control a large number of shares for a relatively small amount of capital. If the stock price increases, the call options can increase in value rapidly, potentially leading to significant profits.

This scheme delivered wins for the earliest retail investors and dealt serious blows to several hedge funds. When these hedge funds saw these positions move against them, they initially tried to increase their short positions, sensing an opportunity. As the retail option buyers piled in, however, the hedging needs of the option market makers selling these options began to drive increased buying of the underlying assets. As the share prices appreciated, another buyer in the form of passive index funds began to buy. GameStop, for example, briefly became the largest stock in the Russell 2000. After selling roughly 18MM shares at an average price of approximately $1.00 in the panic of spring 2020, Vanguard bought just under 4MM shares at an average price of $41.00 per share in the subsequent quarters. As the price rose and rumors of distress spread, other institutions joined the fray, buying more shares.

Unfortunately, without a grounding in either options or fundamentals, most retail investors ended up losing as institutional traders came in and exploited the opportunity. Years later, Twitter and other social media sites continue to be haunted by the painful echoes of this experience.

The Natural Biases of New Traders

Despite the plethora of resources now available via the Internet, investors typically enter the market with only a cursory understanding of options. Their approach is then naturally built around intuition over science, which is easily affected by behavioral biases. Let's break down the two critical behavioral factors that drive retail options trading, so we can ultimately construct a better trading system for beginning options traders.

- Loss Aversion
  The human tendency to avoid catastrophic losses is one of our most central evolutionary traits. We avoid

significant risks, focused on avoiding our demise, in every serious decision.

In options trading, catastrophic loss can only happen when we sell options. Conversely, when we buy options, our maximum loss is fixed. We'll review the payoff diagrams to demonstrate this in Chapter 2.

Additionally, our loss aversion bias leads us to prefer low-price options over more expensive ones.

- Overstating Likelihood of Big Moves

Humans have a well-documented tendency to over-estimate the probability of extreme events occurring (Gonzalez and Wu, 1999). The inflated expectation of low-probability events that can significantly impact prices—such as a company's stock price dramatically increasing due to a favorable earnings report or a ground-breaking new product—drives traders to buy cheap options that are unlikely to be exercised profitably.

Figure 1.2 shows empirical data on the probabilities humans associate (y axis) with events of known probabilities (x axis), as documented by several well-known scientific teams, including the godfathers of Prospect Theory, Kahneman and Tversky. If humans could estimate the probabilities of an event correctly, their guesses would match up with the solid line: a perfect alignment between perceived and actual probabilities. Instead, we see that humans consistently overestimate

Figure 1.2   Human Perception of Probability at Various Levels of Known Probability

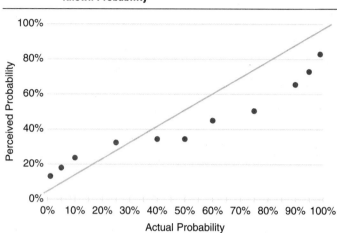

the probabilities of low-likelihood events (dots above the solid line) and underestimate the probability of very likely events (dots below the solid line).

For example, if we look at events with known probability of occurrence of 10%, we see that humans generally perceive the likelihood of that event to be approximately 24%. And if you keep going left on the horizontal axis the relative overestimation gets worse and worse. Events with 1% probability of occurrence are typically estimated at around 13% likelihood, a whopping 13× overestimation. It is this type of gross overestimation of probabilities that can really trip up traders running on pure instinct.

In summary, loss aversion drives traders into buying (not selling) options to avoid risks of unknown loss, and of course, the lower the risk, the better; hence, cheap options appeal to this bias. Then, we layer in the overestimation of low-probability events (e.g., market crash or massive earnings beat). These are situations where the cheapest options are likely the most effective, again pushing the trader into buying the cheapest options.

If this joint bias isn't intuitive, look to your local corner store and check out the latest Powerball or Mega Millions values. These cheap options offer a similar profile to lottery tickets, except outcomes aren't truly random, and the payoffs don't approach 300 million to one.

And those random social media accounts with huge reported profit & loss (P&L) mentioned earlier add fuel to this fire, inspiring new traders to believe that these cheap, high-payoff trades can be profitable in just a few rolls of the dice.

The Amateur Trap

The reason buying cheap options is such a bad idea is that most of them expire worthless. To intuit why, it helps to remember that options are financial instruments with an expiration date. Buying an option is like betting that a specific event will happen within a particular timeframe. If BOTH don't occur, the bet and the money paid to make the bet are lost. In the case of buying stock options, the event is the stock price moving far enough in your favor during the timeframe before the option expires.

Figure 1.3 shows the fraction of 4-week put options at different starting costs (decile 1 being the most expensive and decile 10 being the cheapest) that expire worthless. The horizontal line is the average across all starting costs,

Figure 1.3   Percent of Worthless 4-Week SPY Puts at Expiry at Various Starting Price Deciles; Data from January 2013 to August 2023

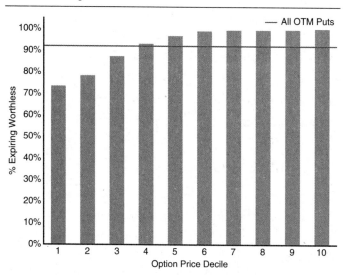

a whopping 92%. If you lose 92% of the time, then just to break even, you need to make slightly more than 12× on your wins (1 divided by 8%). This is challenging.

The situation gets worse for traders looking for low price options to "hit it big." Due to both loss aversion and overestimation of low-probability events, new traders are biased toward cheaper options (think deciles 3 to 7); on average 95% of the options in this cost range expire worthless, requiring winning trades to earn 20× to break even (1 divided by 5%). Following this strategy with smart risk management results in slowly losing money over time. But the inflated probability assigned to these outsized events often makes traders bet more than they should. And instead of slowly losing money, one can lose their money quickly.

We will leave you with a Warren Buffett observation: "Only buy something that you'd be perfectly happy to hold if the market shut down for 10 years." Since an option derives much of its value from time (we'll discuss this in more detail in Chapter 2), buying options cannot meet this good advice.

An Intuitive Conclusion

These factors culminate in a simple fact: the professional trade is to sell options for small, consistent profits. You're taking the reverse side of the typical retail option trade, small income with the potential for large drawdowns—not the most intuitive profile, but the strategy that turns out to be the winning one in most situations. Pursuing the high-probability path, while managing risk, is the focus of this book. In Chapter 3, we will widen our lens to the full options ecosystem to show that selling options is still the optimal path to success, even when considering professional traders on the long side of options.

The allure of options trading is powerful, fueled by tales of overnight riches and financial freedom. However, the reality is that successful options trading requires a comprehensive understanding of the market's intricacies, a solid strategy that tempers our most natural human biases, and meticulous risk management. In subsequent chapters, we will delve deeper into these components to equip you with the knowledge and tools you need for successful options trading.

Chapter Two

The Barebones Option Primer

THE MATHEMATICS OF OPTIONS is complex; the inventors of the sophisticated Black–Merton–Scholes model that underpins most options pricing won the 1997 Nobel Prize in economics. But you don't need this level of mathematics to be a profitable options trader. In this chapter, we will walk you through all the critical elements of options that one needs to understand the remainder of this book.

Key Takeaways:

1. Options are the right to buy (calls) or sell (puts) an underlying asset at a preset price, at or before a prespecified date.

2. At expiration, the value of a call (put) option looks like a hockey stick: worthless below (above) the strike and linearly pays out based on the amount the underlying asset price is above (below) the strike otherwise.

3. Ahead of expiry the hockey stick payoff is smoother, so one can profit off shifts in underlying asset price before expiry or from the passage of time.

4. The value of an option is composed of two components: intrinsic and extrinsic value. Intrinsic value is the option's value if it expires immediately, the "real" value. Extrinsic value is the option's "potential" value, driven by time to expiry, volatility, and distance to strike.

5. Buying and selling options simultaneously creates payoffs that are simple sums of individual option payoff graphs. By mapping these payoffs, we can quickly understand our risks and likely payoffs.

Option Basics

An option is a financial derivative, which means it derives its value from an underlying asset (or "underlier"). This underlying asset can be a stock, a bond, a commodity, a currency, an ETF, or even an index.

An option contract establishes an agreement between two parties: the buyer, who acquires the right granted by the option, and the seller, also known as the writer, who assumes the obligation to fulfill the contract if the buyer chooses to exercise this right. For acquiring this right, the buyer pays a premium to the seller; this premium is the option's price.

Several factors influence the option's price, including the underlying asset's price, time until expiration, and the asset's volatility. But before we understand what affects the price of an option, let's review the fundamental language and mechanics of options.

When traders anticipate an increase in the value of an underlying asset, they can purchase a **call option**. This option gives them the right to buy the asset at a predetermined price, known as the **strike price**, before or at the option's **expiration date**.[1] For instance, if a stock is currently

---

[1] As this book will focus solely on ETF options, we assume exercise can happen at or before expiry, since these are "American" options. This contrasts to "European" options, which can only be exercised at expiration.

trading at $100, and a trader buys a 1-month call option with a strike price of $110, they are betting that the stock price will exceed $110 (plus the premium paid) by the time the option expires in the next month.

Figure 2.1A graphically depicts this scenario at expiry (we will review the payoffs before expiry a bit later). As you can see, once the underlying asset reaches the strike price, the option value grows linearly since the option holder can exercise his right to buy the stock for $110 and immediately sell that stock at the going rate in the market. For example, if the stock price is at $115, the option holder can exercise his right and sell those shares to the market for an instant profit of $115 – $110 (less the premium paid), a linear function of the stock price versus the strike price.

The diagram in Figure 2.1A also shows how the trade is only profitable for the option buyer once the stock price is above the strike by the amount of the premium paid. Since the buyer paid a premium for his option, a sunk cost, the linear payout must surpass this combined level to achieve profitability.

Conversely, a **put option** gives the buyer the right to sell the underlying asset at the strike price, before or at the option's expiry. This type of option is purchased when there is a belief that the asset's price will decline. If the asset's price falls below the strike price, the put option holder can exercise their right to sell the asset at the higher

Figure 2.1 Option Payoff Profile at Expiry

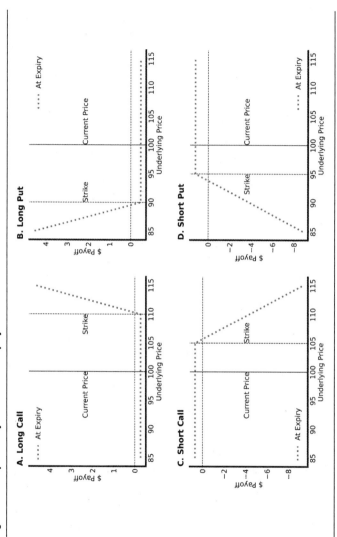

strike price, realizing a profit. Consider a stock priced at $100. If a trader believes its price will fall below $90, they might buy a put option with a $90 strike price. The put option becomes profitable when the stock trades below $90 minus the premium paid, as illustrated in Figure 2.1B. This graphic representation helps traders visualize how a put option becomes profitable.

As mentioned in Chapter 1, the bread-and-butter trade we will focus on in this book is selling options, so we now highlight these payoff structures in Figures 2.1C and D, where the max payoff is now the premium sold, and potential risk is uncapped. The uncapped risk should not feel like a very comfortable trade, given your natural disposition as a human to avoid significant losses and overestimate the likelihood of extreme events, but this is precisely why this trade can win over time.

Options in Time

While the mechanics of option exercise (i.e., exercising the right to buy the underlying asset for the strike price) are at the core of option theory, it won't be an essential feature for us going forward. This is because, as traders, we will not focus on strategies involving buying or selling the underlying asset through option exercise.

Instead, we will only focus on strategies that profit from changes in option values—for example, selling an option for a dollar and then repurchasing it before expiration for a few cents. Now that you understand why option values change with the underlying price due to the ability to exercise, you will no longer need to think about those exercise mechanics, just about the resulting payoff profile as a function of the underlying asset price.

Figure 2.2 now shows the payoff diagrams as a function of time. We see the option's price at entry, halfway from entry to expiry, and finally at expiry (same as Figure 2.1). The major change now is that for most of the time you hold the option, the kink in the payoff is not as sharp as a hockey stick. So, an option owner doesn't necessarily need to wait until the underlier moves from one side of the strike to the other to change profitability.

This is key for traders who are not necessarily holding to expiry or considering exercising. We can profit from a trade without holding until expiry or until crossing strikes.

It's also critical to note that an option typically has a lot of value beyond what it would be worth if it expired today. And this excess value slowly decays over time. So, beyond earning money based on a move in the underlier, one can also make money by selling an option and letting time pass until the time value premium is gone.

Figure 2.2   Option Payoff Profile Before Expiry

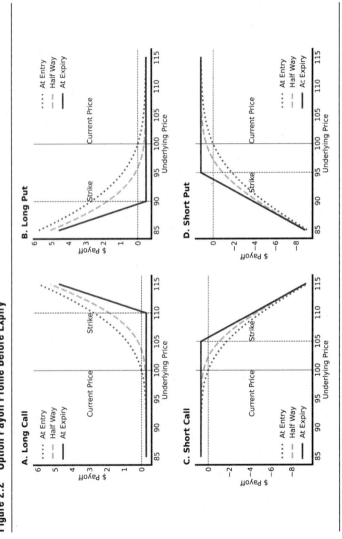

Breaking Down the Option Premium

The value of an option, commonly referred to as the premium, is an amalgamation of two fundamental components: intrinsic value and extrinsic value. Each element plays a crucial role in determining the overall worth of an option contract. Let's delve deeper into what constitutes these values and the factors that influence them. For this example, we will assume the underlying asset of the option is a stock.

Intrinsic Value: The "Real" Value of an Option

Intrinsic value is the "real" value of an option. It represents the immediate, tangible value of the option if exercised immediately. This value is straightforward in its calculation but crucial for understanding how options are valued.

- **Call Options**: The intrinsic value is the difference between the stock's current price and the option's strike price, but only if this value is positive. If the stock's current price is lower than the strike price, the intrinsic value is zero, as exercising the option would not be beneficial. This dynamic is represented by the "At Expiry" hockey stick seen in Figure 2.1A, since the intrinsic value before expiry is the same as the option's total value at expiry.

- **Put Options**: Conversely, the intrinsic value of a put option is the difference between the strike price and the stock's current price, provided this value is positive. If the stock's price is above the strike price, the intrinsic value is zero, as there's no advantage in exercising the option. Again, we see this in the "At Expiry" hockey stick from Figure 2.1B since the intrinsic value before expiry is the same as the option's total value at expiry.

Now is an excellent time to review some essential terms that indicate where the stock price is relative to the option's strike price, which immediately tells you about an option's intrinsic value. **Out-of-the-money (OTM)** options have no intrinsic value, which means the underlying price is below the strike for calls and above the strike for puts. **In-the-money (ITM)** options have positive intrinsic value, which means the price is above the strike for calls and below the strike for puts. Finally, **at-the-money (ATM)** options sit right at the threshold, with no intrinsic value but great potential for this to change with minor underlying price changes. ATM options have a strike that is the same as the underlier price.

The relative location of strike versus price can also be described on a percentage scale known as option **moneyness**. An option where the strike is 5% above the underlying price is said to have a moneyness of 105. Similarly, an option where the strike is 5% below the underlying price has a moneyness of 95. This language is generally the most efficient way to describe option moneyness.

ADULT SWIM: GOING GREEK

Option professionals love to know exactly how fast the price of an option will move relative to the underlying. In option nerd world, this is labeled as Δ (a capital "D" in Greek), called "Delta." It signifies the instantaneous rate of change of option price as the underlying price moves. In calculus, this is simply the first derivative of the option price with respect to the underlier price. In Figure 2.3A, we again show the payoff function for a long call option from Figure 2.2A. In Figure 2.3B we now plot Delta for the long call, where we see Delta evolve from 0 to 1 as the underlying price moves from well below strike to well above strike. If you are comfortable with derivatives, you can easily map Delta by just looking at the slope in Figure 2.3A. As a fun exercise, go ahead and map out what the Delta for a sold call is. And do the same for long and short positions in puts.

Figure 2.3   Call Option Delta and Gamma

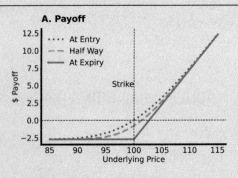

A. Payoff

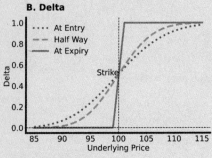

B. Delta

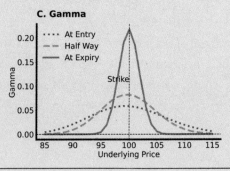

C. Gamma

There are several reasons Delta is useful. First, sometimes people talk about buying options with a specific Delta, not moneyness or strike. For example, instead of buying a 95 moneyness call or a call with 100 strike, one might say they are buying a 20 Delta call, which depends not just on moneyness/strike, but also other variables like time to expiry.

Second, for investors trying to understand how their portfolio will behave relative to the underlying, Delta is the "hedge ratio" of the option. For example, if you buy a 25 Delta call option, the price of the option will rise by 25 cents for the first $1.00 increase in the price of the underlying asset, providing a 25% hedge to a matching position in the underlying.

While we're on the topic of Delta, it's a great time to also mention Γ (capital "G" in Greek), called "Gamma." This is the rate of change of Delta, the first derivative of Delta with respect to underlier price, or the second derivative of option price with respect to underlying price. Gamma tells you how fast Delta itself is changing as the underlying price changes. We plot Gamma in Figure 2.3C for the long call option. As you can see, Gamma peaks near the strike of the option, since this is the highest slope point of the Delta graph in Figure 2.3B. Once again, you can deduce the

Gamma plot by just mapping out the slope of the Delta plot. Finally, since Gamma is always greater than 0 for a long call position, in the above example for a 25 Delta call option, after the first $1.00 price increase, the Delta of the call option will have increased, and the revised hedge ratio will be higher.

Extrinsic Value: The "Potential" Value

Extrinsic value is more complex because it embodies the option's potential. It's not about the option's current value but what it could be worth in the future. The extrinsic value is the amount the option is worth beyond its intrinsic value, which is the gap between the option payoffs of Figure 2.1 from some time before expiry to the "At Expiry" hockey stick. Let's review the three most important factors in determining extrinsic value: time to expiry, volatility, and distance to strike.

1. **Time to Expiry**: A key driving factor of extrinsic value is the time to expiry. The longer the time until expiration, the greater the chance the underlying asset's price could move in a favorable direction, increasing the option's value. One can see this vividly in Figure 2.2, where the price of the option goes up as one is further from expiry, even when there is no

intrinsic value (the option is OTM). The component of extrinsic value that is driven by the time to expiry is known as **time value**. Time value decreases as the option approaches its expiration, a phenomenon known as time decay. Also, time value is highest when strike is near the underlying price, since this is where the possibility of a win that is not a win yet is highest.

2. **Volatility**: Volatility measures how much the underlying asset's price is expected to fluctuate over a certain period. This metric is almost always expressed in annualized terms, representing the expected standard deviation of price changes over the course of one year. Higher volatility means a greater range of potential movement for the underlying asset, which increases the chances that the option could end up ITM. As such, options on volatile assets typically command higher premiums.

   Implied volatility (IV) is the future volatility currently assumed in an option price. One can accurately find this number because all other data points used to formally price an option, like the underlier price and time to expiry, are known. Since this book is all about building an option selling strategy, we will ultimately be focused on selling options with implied volatility higher than we expect to be realized over our holding period. Much more on that later, though.

3. **Distance to Strike**: The further the underlying price is below (above) the strike for a call (put), the lower the probability of the option ending with significant value. Hence, the extrinsic value will be low. Similarly, if the underlying price is way above (below) the strike for a call (put), there is little excess potential for the option beyond the intrinsic value; hence, once again the extrinsic value is low. But when an option is close to ATM, then the option has incredible potential based on possible near-term market movements, and it has high extrinsic value. This dynamic is starkly visible when comparing option payoffs in Figure 2.2 ahead of expiry and at expiry.

There are a couple of crucial things to note now that we understand intrinsic versus extrinsic value. First is that there are two simple ways an option seller can make money. The underlying price could move further OTM in a second, a minute, or any time before expiry—which leads to a drop in extrinsic value since the strike is further away now. Or the underlier of an option could barely move, and time can just elapse, evaporating any extrinsic value that the seller took in as a sold premium.

The second key takeaway is that the higher the volatility, the higher the option premium received due to increased extrinsic value. When you sell options, you will generally be looking for higher IV options as long as their realized volatility is expected to be lower than what's implied.

Finally, moneyness is a key determinant of the fraction of your option premium at risk due to time decay. ITM options are dominated by intrinsic value, leaving little exposure to time decay, and are viewed by many to be "safer" due to the lack of this risk. In contrast, OTM options are comprised purely of extrinsic value and are "riskier" for buyers since there is a significant chance of losing the entire premium via time decay.

These OTM options are also generally lower priced and offer more leverage to the buyer. As noted earlier, amateur traders are naturally drawn to buying OTM options with their lower premiums and potential for high payouts on low-probability outcomes, and we will generally take the other side of this trade. Our objective is to harvest sizable extrinsic value in a risk-managed way.

Combining Options

Rather than sell a single option, we recommend combining options into trading packages. We will focus on this for our core trades in this book, so let's now review how one constructs payoffs when simultaneously buying and selling two options.

Figure 2.4A shows the payoff when we buy a call with a $105 strike and sell a call at a $110 strike, known as a

Figure 2.4   Summing Option Payoffs

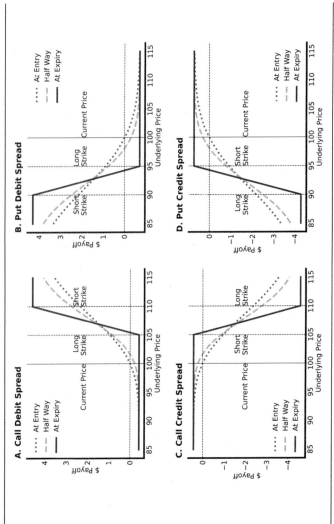

call debit spread. You see that the upside is now capped, but the price you paid for this package is less than if you just bought the $105 call, since you took in a premium when you sold the $110 strike. To practice nomenclature here, the moneyness of this call spread is 105–110, since it just so happens that the purchased call is 5% OTM and the sold call is 10% OTM. The term "debit" refers to the fact that we owe a net premium. If we reversed the trade, sold the $105, and bought the $110, we would almost certainly have received a "credit" for the trade. Again, this will factor into our core trading profile.

Figure 2.4B shows the payoff when you buy a put and then sell a further out-of-the-money put (**put debit spread**), again capping the potential reward but paying less for the package. The key thing to notice about these spread payoffs is that they are **simply the sum of the payoffs of the individual legs**. Take a second to draw it out for yourself on paper to grasp this approach's simplicity.

Figures 2.4C and D highlight the payoffs of the above two packages for the seller (denoted as **credit spreads**), where we now see something critical: selling credit spreads now caps our max loss, unlike selling single ("naked") calls or puts. This risk management feature will be a key part of our options selling strategy: we will sell spreads, rather than single options, to limit our potential max loss.

You are likely familiar with the name Nassim Taleb, whose books *Fooled by Randomness* and *The Black Swan* anticipated the challenges of the Global Financial Crisis. Nassim's work highlights the unknown probabilities of extreme events—the proverbial "Black Swan" or "Left Tail"—and cautions against the risks of selling these low-price options.

We share his concerns and would highlight that few retail investors are truly equipped to "sell the tail." You can certainly make money over shorter lengths of time, but the risk of ruin is high if you pursue the strategy for any extended period of time. In other words, even though we advise against buying these options to generate profits, their value as protection in your portfolio can still be positive.

By converting to a put spread from simply selling outright puts, we are "buying back" that extreme risk. There are times when it may make sense to sell the put outright or even buy the put, and we'll explore some situations where this makes sense in later chapters. But for now, we want to emphasize that if you'd like to sleep well at night, "Don't leave your tail exposed!"

You are now armed with all the basics you need to create a winning options trading framework. Let's solidify our knowledge of option basics through a few examples.

Real-World Examples

Example 1: ITM Call Options—Apple Inc. (AAPL)

Scenario: Imagine Apple Inc. (AAPL) stock is trading at $150. A trader buys a call option that expires in 1 month, with a strike price of $145, for a price of $5.50.

Intrinsic Value: The intrinsic value of this call option is the difference between the current stock price ($150) and the strike price ($145), which is $5. This means that if the option were exercised immediately, it would be worth $5 per share, or $500 per contract (as each standard contract represents 100 shares).

Real-World Context: This could occur before a major product announcement from Apple, where the trader anticipates an increase in the stock's value due to positive consumer and investor reaction, but doesn't want to make a very risky bet. By buying an option dominated by intrinsic value, he isn't requiring a move beyond the small extrinsic value of $0.50 to have a profitable trade. This isn't particularly interesting to option sellers given the lack of extrinsic value.

Example 2: OTM Call Options—Tesla Inc. (TSLA)

Scenario: Tesla Inc. (TSLA) stock is trading at $600. A trader buys an out-of-the-money (OTM) call option with a strike price of $650 that expires in 3 months. The option's premium is $20.

Extrinsic Value and Time Decay: Since the call option is OTM, its intrinsic value is $0. The entire premium of $20 is thus extrinsic value. As the expiration date approaches, and if Tesla's stock price remains below $650, the extrinsic value (and thus the premium) will decrease due to time decay.

Real-World Context: Such a situation might happen when investors expect significant growth from Tesla, perhaps due to anticipated government policy changes favoring electric vehicles. Here the trader is expecting an outsized move, and is willing to bet that the option, which is currently OTM, will become ITM with ease. And if this happens, the investor gets compensated nicely because right now there is no intrinsic value, but once ITM there would be. Option sellers love selling these since they expire worthless most of the time, but sellers need to make sure they are protected from a skyrocketing TSLA price.

Example 3: ATM Call Options—Pfizer Inc. (PFE)

Scenario: In the lead-up to Pfizer announcing successful COVID-19 vaccine trial results, the stock is trading with heightened volatility, and a trader goes long ATM calls that will be profitable at expiration if PFE moves higher by more than the premium paid.

Extrinsic Value: The options on Pfizer stocks would have seen an increase in premiums due to the high volatility. An investor purchasing options before the announcement would pay more due to the uncertainty and potential for a significant stock price movement. This is all extrinsic value since these are ATM.

Real-World Context: This scenario played out in late 2020, as pharmaceutical companies like Pfizer were in the race to develop a COVID-19 vaccine. The news of successful trials led to significant stock movements. This is potentially a great opportunity for option sellers to come in if they believe the implied volatility is significantly above potential future volatility, creating excess amounts of extrinsic value that can potentially be harvested. However, most volatility sellers would avoid being too close to ATM given the significant probability of the option moving against them so close to being ATM.

Chapter Three

Become the House

———————— ～ ————————

UP TO NOW WE have spent time motivating the reader to consider selling options instead of buying them. We have also armed readers with the essential foundational knowledge needed to create a smart option strategy. In this chapter we will further justify selling options by expanding our lens to the broader option ecosystem and carefully examining the empirical data. We will then present the core option trade we want our readers to master. This will be the option-selling template we build on throughout the rest of the book.

Key Takeaways:

1. Professional investors buy options for hedging or to obtain non-recourse leverage. The participation of these parties enormously expands the pool of capital that we can sell options to.
2. By selling options we have effectively entered three businesses where we are "the house": a casino, an insurance company, and a bank.
3. Our bread-and-butter trade is selling SPY put spreads, where we act as an insurance company, and earn both liquidity premia and bias premia.
4. In a historical context, selling 2-week 90–96 SPY put spreads wins 95% of the time without taking excessive risks, and is a great representation of the core "insurance company" trade we want the reader to focus on.

The Broader Option Ecosystem

Chapter 1 began with a review of the biases of novice traders, where we noted that human behavior favors buying cheaper, OTM options. We also used this lens to convince our readers newer to trading that it is wiser to sell into these biases, taking the other side of the trade and selling these options instead of buying them. Let's now expand these perspectives to account for all the different players buying options, including seasoned individuals, financial advisors, pensions, hedge funds, and more.

Hedgers and speculators are the key buyers of options. A hedger purchases options to insulate some of the losses they would experience in an adverse move against their underlying holding. In general, just as with any other insurance policy, the hedger hopes the insurance is never needed, so the expectation is that the purchased option will lose money while they make money on the underlier.

In contrast, a speculator is different since they typically will not hold the underlier. Unlike the hedger, their hope is to make money on the option position; but what's interesting is that the speculator also generally expects to lose money on the option. While the speculator expects to lose frequently when buying these options, they expect to make large profits when they do win, which would more than cover the frequent small losses.

Hedging example: If I own Apple (AAPL) shares and believe the long-term prospects for the stock are good, but I am concerned about the upcoming earnings report, I might buy short-dated, inexpensive put options to protect my portfolio against an extreme move. I have bought insurance on my AAPL stock.

Speculator example: I do not currently have a position in XYZ Biotech (a promising company holding the key to the secrets of the alphabet), but I've received a "hot tip" from my online friend Jimmy2Cats that XYZ will be acquired. Since I don't know XYZ Biotech very well, I decide to buy a low-price, out-of-the-money call option on XYZ. My losses are limited, and my potential payout is huge. I have bought a lottery ticket, and if Jimmy is correct, we'll celebrate together. If he's wrong, I'll have lost very little and can sympathize with Jimmy2Cats at low cost.

Both buyers are spending money they expect to lose. The hedger expects to make money on her stock while losing money on the option. The speculator expects to lose a small amount, but if Jimmy2Cats is right, he can make a lot. In both situations, as the option seller, we will be paid for providing market liquidity as well as for an extra bias premium associated with loss aversion and overstated probabilities of extreme events. In this framework, retail traders typically fall in the speculator camp, and professionals typically fall under the hedger framework.

Let's rephrase this situation. If you think about it, buying cheap options is akin to sitting at a roulette table or holding a lotto ticket. You're making small bets for potential big payouts. Hence, when you're selling options to this part of the option ecosystem, you are acting like a casino. And casinos are a very lucrative business. But we also must note that it's a business of numbers, and the casino exploits their edge ruthlessly. While there are always periods when casinos might be losing, in the long run the casino always wins. This is exactly how you want to approach selling options. Be the house!

As noted earlier, professional investors are also big buyers of OTM options for hedging purposes. There is demand for both equity and bond puts, used to hedge portfolios from both equity and interest rate risks. Here you are playing to the exact same biases as described in Chapter 1 (loss aversion and overestimation of low-probability events); they just take a different form. Amateur traders have cash and want to hit some home runs, so they are more focused on buying single-name stock puts and calls, which have the chance of overnight riches with one good corporate announcement. On the other hand, professional hedgers have an existing equity and bond portfolio they need to hedge. For example, they are buying puts on equity indices or ETFs, such as the S&P 500 and SPY (the SPDR S&P 500 ETF), respectively.

When we are selling options to hedgers, we have now expanded our business empire into the insurance world! Again, just like casinos, insurance companies can lose money over short periods, but over the long run, if they take appropriate measures to manage risk, they come out ahead because humans will pay a premium for this service that they know on average they won't recoup.

It turns out there is one more business we are going to get into as option sellers: banking. This is because professional investors also use call options for getting leverage beyond a cash position. Here, we no longer benefit from core human biases of loss aversion and low-probability overestimation. Now, we are being paid to be a lender. We still earn a premium, but it will be a bit less since there isn't a core bias embedded in this trade. Since these investors also begin with a diversified portfolio of equities and bonds, we will see this play out when we sell calls on indices and ETFs that match the holdings in the portfolio, things like SPY and TLT (the iShares 20+ Year Treasury Bond ETF).

As you will see in Chapter 5, it is more profitable to sell options that hinge on biases, since you earn both a liquidity service premium as well as a behavioral bias premium. This will tilt us toward selling things like equity index puts, bond index puts, and single-name calls (which are unfortunately outside the scope of this book).

Now that we see the full scope of where this is going, let's step back and review the core trade we will be using, and then for the remainder of the book, build off this foundation into a diversified portfolio of option writing.

Our Core Trade

The two critical lessons we learned about selling options in Chapter 2 are:

1. Sell OTM options because they are entirely comprised of extrinsic value.
2. Sell spreads to cap your risk.

We want to sell spreads that are out of the money—it's as simple as that.

Figure 3.1 shows the payoff of an OTM put spread on SPY. SPY is trading at $415, and the spread shown has 2 weeks to expiry, where a put is sold at $398 (96 moneyness) and a put is bought at $373 (90 moneyness). The premium we take in here is $1.37, while risking a worst-case loss of $23.63, which only occurs if we still hold the option at expiry and the price is below $373.

Figure 3.2 shows the results of a strategy that sells this 2W 90–96 SPY put spread every Friday, with a max risk of 100bps[1] to the portfolio. The 100bps max risk to the portfolio (size of $P) is set by selling the number of spreads, where if the max possible loss is realized on the spread, the portfolio

---

[1] A basis point (bp) is 1/100th of a percent. Instead of writing 0.01% we will write 1bp. Plural is basis points (bps).

Figure 3.1   Selling an OTM SPY Put Spread

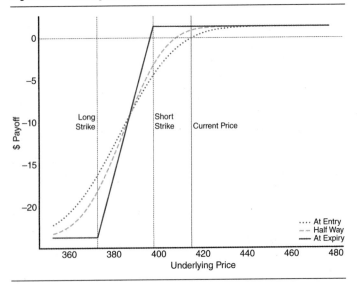

Figure 3.2   2W 90–96 SPY Put Spread Strategy; January 1, 2013 – August 31, 2023

	2W 90–96 SPY Put Spread
Win Rate	94.8%
Mean Win	4.4bps
Mean Loss	−45.2bps

will lose precisely 100bps. The formula we need to solve to find the number of contracts (X) to sell for the example of Figure 3.1 is 100bps = (X * 100 * \$23.63) / \$P. Of course, X will change every time we sell a new spread, since the max loss on that spread will be different and the portfolio size will be different. The strategy is run from January 1, 2013, to August 30, 2023, and will be the backtesting range used throughout this book. As you can see, the strategy wins around 95% of the time, averaging small wins every 2 weeks, with the occasional loss that is on average about half of the max possible loss. This profile agrees nicely with our analogy to being an insurance company when we sell these equity ETF puts.

While this strategy is a net winner, we certainly want to consider ways to lower the mean (average) loss without lowering the win rate or mean win substantially. This is the topic of Chapter 4. But first, let's explain how we came up with the particulars of the above strategy, including the specific strikes traded and the expiry.

Strike Selection

Figure 3.3 shows statistics of all possible permutations of strikes for a 2-week SPY put spread strategy. When you study this, you see that you want to avoid the top left of the matrix

Figure 3.3   Primary Selection Criteria for Selling SPY Put Spreads (2w); January 1, 2013 – August 31, 2023

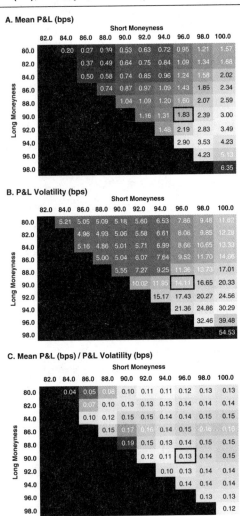

A. Mean P&L (bps)

B. P&L Volatility (bps)

C. Mean P&L (bps) / P&L Volatility (bps)

Figure 3.3 (Continued)

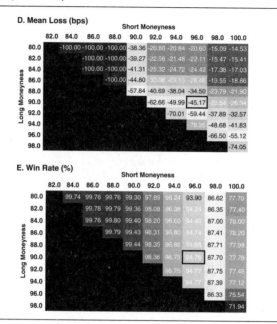

D. Mean Loss (bps)

Short Moneyness (columns); Long Moneyness (rows)

Long \ Short	82.0	84.0	86.0	88.0	90.0	92.0	94.0	96.0	98.0	100.0
80.0		-100.00	-100.00	-100.00	-38.36	-20.86	-20.84	-20.60	-15.09	-14.53
82.0			-100.00	-100.00	-39.27	-22.56	-21.48	-22.11	-15.47	-15.41
84.0				-100.00	-41.31	-25.32	-24.72	-24.42	-17.38	-17.03
86.0					-44.80	-30.06	-29.15	-28.46	-19.55	-18.86
88.0					-57.84	-40.69	-38.04	-34.50	-23.79	-21.90
90.0						-62.66	-49.99	-45.17	-29.54	-26.34
92.0							-70.01	-59.44	-37.89	-32.57
94.0								-78.35	-48.68	-41.83
96.0									-66.50	-55.12
98.0										-74.05

E. Win Rate (%)

Short Moneyness (columns); Long Moneyness (rows)

Long \ Short	82.0	84.0	86.0	88.0	90.0	92.0	94.0	96.0	98.0	100.0
80.0		99.74	99.76	99.76	99.30	97.89	96.24	93.90	86.62	77.70
82.0			99.78	99.79	99.36	98.08	96.38	94.24	86.35	77.40
84.0			99.76	99.80	99.40	98.20	96.60	94.40	87.00	78.00
86.0				99.79	99.43	98.31	96.80	94.74	87.41	78.20
88.0					99.44	98.35	96.68	94.68	87.71	77.98
90.0						98.36	96.75	94.76	87.70	77.76
92.0							96.75	94.77	87.75	77.48
94.0								94.77	87.39	77.12
96.0									86.33	75.54
98.0										71.94

since the returns (Panel A) are quite low, which intuitively makes sense since you are selling spreads so far OTM that they are bringing in almost no premium. On the flipside, though, you don't want to sell spreads in the bottom right because their volatility (Panel B) is high. The sweet spot lies somewhere in the middle between these extremes, which we see to a degree when we consider the ratio of mean P&L to P&L volatility (Panel C).

Now you will also notice that the tighter you go on strikes in the bottom left of that middle zone, you end up having large mean losses (Panel D). This might be okay for you—it completely depends on your requirements—but we prefer to steer away from that kind of profile since most clients will not enjoy the feeling of large losses when they occur. At the same time, if you go too wide in strikes, the top right of the matrix, your win rate (Panel E) goes down. That's also not optimal in our opinion for a strategy like this, since clients expect it to be a consistent winner.

A black box highlights the 90–96 spread. This is our view of the "sweet" spot for this type of trade. But as we've mentioned, this is greatly driven by our utility function as an investor, which could be quite different from yours. As you gain experience trading these kinds of spreads, you will naturally find your own sweet spot, and you should evolve your strike selection accordingly. For example, you might prefer less volatility than we have chosen here; or you may want to reach for higher returns at the cost of higher mean losses. You will only understand your personal sweet spot after trading this strategy for a while, taking careful note of your own biases and how you psychologically respond to both winning and losing trades.

Before we move on, let us emphasize that this sweet spot is not permanent. The discussion above was a historical study to frame strike selection. We would only trade these precise strikes if markets today aligned perfectly with history. So do not assume the strikes chosen based off history are always what you will focus on. In Chapter 6 we will review our option screening process and show how strikes can be selected in real time.

Expiry Selection

Figure 3.4 shows the mean returns of strategies run with different expiries (1w, 2w, 4w, 6w), where the strikes at each expiry are chosen to match the volatility of our core 2w 90–96 strategy, so that the comparison can cleanly isolate the effects of different expiries. As you can see, the shorter the time to expiry, the greater the average returns.

It turns out that options lose time value nonlinearly. They lose more of their time value just before expiry than they do well before the expiry date. Figure 3.5 highlights the value of an option from 6 weeks to expiry all the way to expiry. Focusing on the ATM position, where the premium is

Figure 3.4   Mean P&L for Different Expiries—Strikes Set to Match 2w 90–96 Volatility: 92–98 for 1w, 88–94 for 4w, and 86–92 for 6w; January 1, 2013 – August 31, 2023

	1W	2W	4W	6W
Mean Weekly P&L	1.43bps	0.91bps	0.75bps	0.57bps

Figure 3.5   Time Decay of a Put Option

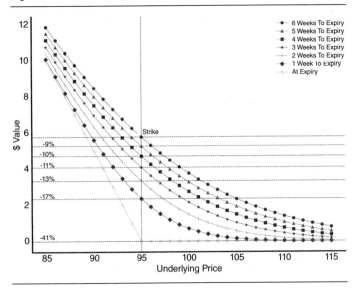

comprised entirely of extrinsic value, we see that in the last 2 weeks the option loses almost the same amount of value that it loses during the 4 weeks before that, a very nonlinear time decay.

We chose 2-week expiries for our core trade, but as you can see, one can earn even more if they consistently sold 1-week spreads. While the product is too new for extensive backtesting, even higher profits can be gained from selling "zero day to expiry" (0DTE) options. Readers of this book are likely familiar with the even more explosive growth of these "same day" options, and hopefully understand why: they are very profitable to sell!

We chose to sell 2-week spreads for operational reasons. For most retail participants, there is a fine line between the operational burden and the potential P&L. But if you have the coding skills, you should consider approaches that incorporate even shorter-dated options—again, "be the house" and take as many bets as you can operationally when the odds are this far in your favor.

As you will see later in this book, we will end up focusing on diversified portfolios of option writing, hence our operational burden will scale just from expanding our underlier universe. We do not want to have to trade weekly with this diversified option writing process, as it would be too operationally intensive.

ADULT SWIM: MORE GREEKS

Our core focus in this book is to make money by selling options and watching their value go to zero. As such, we are very interested in how fast an option decays. In option nerd world this is labeled as Θ, for the Greek letter "Theta." It is the rate of change of option price with the passage of time. Again, this is yet another first derivative of the option price, in this case with respect to time. Theta is generally reported in units of dollars/ day or bps/day, hence it is the premium a trader should expect an option to lose over the course of 1 day, if nothing else changes, i.e., underlying price, implied volatility, etc. are unchanged.

In Figure 3.6 we plot Theta as a function of both time to expiry and underlying price, for the same long put position discussed in Figure 3.5. The two core features of Theta we would like the reader to walk away with are (1) its highest ATM and tails off as you get

Figure 3.6   Theta of a Put Option

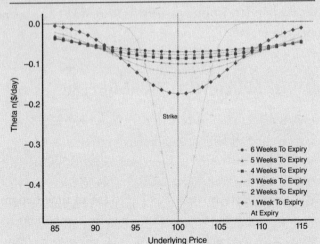

further from strike, and (2) its highest closer to expiry. We encourage the reader to look back to Figure 3.5 and see if they can roughly match these two critical characteristics of Theta from the raw payoff graphs in time we showed there.

Equity ETF Puts for the Win

The mechanics just described for selling spreads (puts or calls) can be applied to any underlying indices, ETFs, and even single-name stocks. In fact, in Chapter 5 we will focus on the diversifying benefits of writing options, both puts and calls, across several underliers. We will also show that spread premia ebb and flow with changing market dynamics, so it's best to have a deep bench of different candidates to be able to generate income consistently.

Focusing on SPY put spreads in this core trade chapter was not random. As we already discussed, SPY put spreads are the favored vehicle for professional investors, a massive pool of capital seeking hedges. To add more demand, equity risk is typically the largest risk in investor portfolios, so if investors are going to spend time hedging any part of their portfolio, it's the equity component. As a result, SPY puts are often an optimal place to be from a demand standpoint.

Additionally, SPY put spreads have a behavioral tailwind in their premia since they involve both loss aversion and overestimation of low-probability events. As we will see in Chapter 5 as we consider other underliers, SPY put spreads are usually the most attractive opportunity when limiting yourself to the most liquid, well-behaved opportunities.

Chapter Four

Risk Management

———— ❧ ————

In Chapter 3 we reviewed our bread-and-butter trade, selling an OTM 2-week SPY put spread. There, we saw that by careful selection of strikes, we could create a profile that has a consistently high win rate with manageable downside risk. In this chapter, we review some risk management tools that can help make this core trade even more attractive.

Key Takeaways:

1. Utilizing stop losses can dramatically lower the mean loss of the strategy without compromising returns.

2. Set stops at a nice middle ground: too tight and it's death by a thousand cuts; too loose, and you don't limit the big losses.

3. For our 90–96 strikes, an at-the-money stop loss is optimal. The put spreads are bought back if the price touches the strike of the sold option.

4. Rolling options "down and out" after they are closed by an ATM stop loss is a powerful way to enhance the strategy, shifting the probabilities in your favor.

5. Historically, it is optimal to roll if there are more than 10 days to expiry of the closed position, a balance between capturing elevated IVs and minimizing exposure to downward momentum.

Moving Beyond "Sell and Hold"

In Figure 4.1 we once again report the summary statistics of our core trade.[1] As a reminder, we sold 2-week (2w) 90–96 SPY put spreads risking 100bps (1%) of the portfolio per sold spread, and we held these spreads to expiry. But there is no reason we can't close these positions before expiry.

Stepping back for a minute, it's important to note that most short-term traders don't have the luxury of prede-fined max losses and max profits. For those traders, limiting

Figure 4.1   2W 90–96 SPY Put Spread Strategy; January 1, 2013 – August 31, 2023

Mean P&L (bps)	1.81
P&L Volatility (bps)	14.05
Mean P&L (bps) / P&L Volatility (bps)	0.13
Mean Loss (bps)	−44.65
Win Rate (%)	94.7

[1] The results in Figure 4.1 are ever so slightly different than the ones shown in Figure 3.3. In chapter 3 we had a large set of possible trades to analyze, so for speed we used our lighter-weight testing environment. In Figure 4.1 we move to our heavyweight minute-interval backtesting system, which will enable us to study risk management tools like the ones reviewed in this chapter. The slight discrepancies seen are due to tiny differences in the way these different systems process the raw source data from the Options Price Reporting Authority.

downside risk and disciplined harvesting of gains are mandatory requirements of their strategy. But it turns out that some of those tools to limit risk and enhance profitability can also be valuable to us.

There are two core risk management tools traders use to exit a trade that protect from downside risks and lock in profits: stop-loss orders and take-profit orders. In this chapter, we will review each of these tools and see if they can enhance our OTM SPY spread writing strategy.

Stop Losses

The first tool, and the most important one that we will consider for our strategy, is a **stop loss**. This is simply a standing order to close a position at a preset price when the trade goes against you. This type of exit trade aims to prevent losses greater than a set amount. By only writing spreads, we have already capped our losses to a preset amount, but now we will explore the use of stop losses well before we reach the max loss potential from our spread if simply sold and held.

Figure 4.2 shows the results of implementing a stop loss on our core SPY writing strategy. Let's start on the far right of Figure 4.2, where we see the results of our strategy with no stop loss. Then moving over one column to the left, we see the results when we close our positions early if the price declines 4% past our sold strike, which we label as 4% ITM. In this case, since we are selling a 90–96 put spread, the spot

Figure 4.2   Stop Loss Impact on 2W 90–96 SPY Put Spread Strategy; January 1, 2013 – August 31, 2023

	2% OTM	ATM	2% ITM	4% ITM	None
Mean P&L (bps)	1.14	1.68	1.74	1.74	1.81
P&L Volatility (bps)	6.25	7.89	11.63	12.97	14.05
Mean P&L (bps) / P&L Volatility (bps)	0.18	0.21	0.15	0.13	0.13
Mean Loss (bps)	-7.52	-17.04	-33.45	-41.42	-44.65
Win Rate (%)	76.64	88.85	93.24	94.33	94.70

price would have had to go down 8% for the sold spread to be 4% ITM. As you see, the statistics don't dramatically change relative to the no stop loss strategy, since this stop loss is barely ever hit. As you move further to the left in Figure 4.2 we are closing positions earlier and earlier during an SPY drawdown. The figure ends with a stop loss rule where we close the spread when spot price is still 2% away from our sold strike, a very tight stop loss.

The tighter you bring in the stop loss (moving right to left), the smaller the mean loss since you are getting out of positions moving against you earlier and earlier. At the same time, your volatility is going down, since you avoid large potential losses. However, your returns are dropping, and your win rate is decreasing. If one considers the risk-adjusted return in the third row of Figure 4.2, defined here as the mean P&L/P&L volatility, there is clearly a sweet spot near ATM stop loss where this metric peaks. This is fortunate since an ATM stop loss will also be very useful for avoiding "assignment," as discussed in Chapter 6.

Even more important to us than lowering volatility is reducing our mean loss. Layering in an ATM stop loss cuts the mean loss by over 60% (−44.65bps to −17.04bps) while only reducing the mean P&L by around 9% (1.81bps to 1.68bps), a risk management home run that we will use from here on out:

Use an ATM stop loss, which closes the spread when underlying price hits the sold strike.

Let us digress and provide an important tale of warning. One of the most common mistakes new traders make is setting stop losses too tight, an intuitive consequence of the loss aversion bias reviewed in Chapter 1. But this ultra conservative strategy will inevitably lead to getting "paper cut to death," whereby a trader sustains small losses repeatedly until their account goes to zero. For example, if we continued Figure 4.2 even further to the left, say to 3% OTM stop loss, mean P&L would drop to 0.60bps; and if we went to say a 4% OTM stop, mean P&L would be 0.24bps, likely insufficient to cover your costs for running the strategy!

Peeling the onion back one step further to really hammer this home, besides the use of spreads, the intelligent application of stop losses is the most important risk management tool to take away from this book. We earn money selling these SPY put spreads because we are providing a service.

Specifically, we are selling insurance. To earn the full premium, you need to hold this insurance policy for most of the period through expiry. You must genuinely bear the risk that the put buyer wants you to hedge for them: a move against their long equity position sometime during the life of the option. If you consistently close your position at the first sign of risk, you will not earn this premium because you are not ultimately providing an insurer's service. Ironically, you're doing the opposite—buying insurance on your insurance at the first sign of trouble!

And now one final warning on this subject. You might think that you could just leverage the aggressive stop strategy to earn sufficient amounts, say the 3% OTM stop strategy with a mean P&L of 0.60bps. The problem with this idea is that stops can be missed! Typically, they aren't, but if there's a fast enough market move (e.g., a war breaking out), your stops can be missed. In this scenario, a highly levered position could be down the full risk exposure in an instant, a much larger loss than you would experience with a less levered position!

Before we move on to our next risk management tool, we want to remind the reader that the ATM stop loss is only being recommended for the specific 90–96 strike combination we are using. If you decide to sell at something other than a 96 moneyness, you are changing the frequency at which the sold strike is getting hit, and hence changing the value of the stop loss. Remember that stop losses that are too tight (i.e., hitting too frequently) were suboptimal. So, if you decide to sell at 98 moneyness, and use an ATM stop, you will be stopped out all the time, lowering the profitability of your strategy significantly.

Profit Taking

The other common risk management technique used by traders is to close a trade at a preset profitability level. This is effectively the exact same concept as a stop loss, except now we close early when we have a targeted gain rather than a loss. It's understandable that we want to ensure that a winning trade is booked as a win rather than be exposed to that final "flip of the coin." If the "too tight" stop loss can be compared to buying back insurance at the first sign of trouble, the systematic gain harvesting can be thought of as buying back that insurance when others are willing to sell it to you at a lower price. As Warren Buffett notes about the insurance business (Buffett, n.d.):

> There are only two reasons for buying insurance.
> First is to protect yourself against losses you
> are unwilling or unable to bear. The second is
> because you think the insurance company is
> selling the insurance too cheaply.

Figure 4.3 Profit Taking Effects on Core SPY 2W 90–96 Put Spread Strategy; January 1, 2013 – August 31, 2023

	50%	70%	90%	95%	None
Mean P&L (bps)	1.64	1.60	1.61	1.75	1.81
P&L Volatility (bps)	10.17	12.55	13.88	13.94	14.05
Mean P&L (bps) / P&L Volatility (bps)	0.16	0.13	0.12	0.13	0.13
Mean Loss (bps)	-65.72	-57.41	-45.92	-45.86	-44.65
Win Rate (%)	98.19	96.74	94.93	94.93	94.70

Figure 4.3 shows the results of closing our SPY 2W 90–96 put spread once we have taken in a set percentage of the maximum possible payoff from our spread. For example, the "None" column allows the strategy to be held to maturity in all situations. The 95% column is where we sell, for example, a $1 put spread (the max possible profit), and we close it when it is only worth $.05. We could have held it all the way to expiry and made an additional 5 cents (the "None" column), but we have chosen to close it early to lock in a target profit. The 50% column means we would take profits once we've achieved 50% of our maximum profit level (i.e., 50 cents).

The core observation from Figure 4.3 is that early profit-taking detracts from returns without substantially lowering volatility or mean losses. If you buy back the spread close to your max profitability (e.g., 95% profitability level), you are leaving a few pennies on the table with low risk of being adversely hit by that position. On the other hand, if you close the trade even earlier (e.g., at 50% of max profit), you bring your win rate up, while your mean P&L seems to decline by very little, a potentially interesting outcome. The challenge here is that your mean loss increases, and your return and risk statistics are worse than just implementing an ATM stop loss (illustrated in Figure 4.2).

What about if you layer profit-taking on top of our preferred ATM stop-loss rule—is there possibly a benefit from combining these tools together? Figure 4.4 shows the results. Now you see an even more severe deterioration of the P&L than we saw in Figure 4.3 as you focus on tighter profit-taking rules (left side of Figure 4.4).

Implementing profit-taking rules will be tempting since they let you take risk off the table. You must remember that this is a losing proposition for two key reasons. First, both the ATM stop-loss rule and the use of put spreads are huge layers of protection; you must always remember that you are not generally facing max loss risk with a stop-loss exit strategy in place. Second, when the trade is moving in your favor

Figure 4.4 Profit Taking Effects on Core SPY 2W 90–96 Put Spread Strategy with ATM Stop Loss; January 1, 2013 – August 31, 2023

	50%	70%	90%	95%	None
Mean P&L (bps)	1.14	1.40	1.51	1.63	1.68
P&L Volatility (bps)	6.30	7.13	7.68	7.78	7.89
Mean P&L (bps) / P&L Volatility (bps)	0.18	0.20	0.20	0.21	0.21
Mean Loss (bps)	-19.03	-18.16	-17.12	-17.15	-17.04
Win Rate (%)	93.12	91.12	89.13	89.13	88.85

(becoming more profitable), the further away it is from being a severe downside risk to your portfolio. There is both less time for the position to move against you and the underlying price has risen to the point that the likelihood of a large enough SPY move is very low.

In this configuration, both the put that you own and the put that you have sold are the extreme tails described by Nassim Taleb. These tails carry significant value and as our empirical results demonstrate, you reduce your returns by buying back these extreme risks. As long as you have properly managed your aggregate exposure, your portfolio is protected from catastrophic outcomes while benefiting from the remaining decay in these options.

Rolling Positions

We have found that stop losses are a powerful risk mitigator for our OTM spread writing while profit-taking doesn't seem to add much value. But there is an important notion we have glossed over thus far. When we closed a position early, we did not establish new positions during the remaining time until the expiry of the closed spread. We simply waited to sell once again our 2W 90–96 SPY put spread.

For many, not reinvesting after a stop loss is a welcome pause after an unexpected bout of volatility. It feels very natural to stand aside and see how the next few weeks play out.

"What's the harm if I miss out on the next week or so a few times once in a while?" Spoiler alert: it's quite suboptimal to stay on the sidelines!

Figure 4.5 shows what happens to our core strategy, now using an ATM stop loss, if we sell again when there are a certain number of days left before our next natural sell date. This process is known as "rolling down and out," since you are restriking "down" 4% in moneyness, and you are rolling "out" to a new expiry that is 2 weeks from today.

Starting from the right of Figure 4.5 we see our core strategy with ATM stop loss and no rolling of closed positions. The "12D" column next to it is the same strategy, but we now roll down and out if positions are stopped out more than 12 calendar days from their expiry. In other words, if our position is closed within the first 2 days of holding it, we will roll into a new spread.

You significantly improve the strategy by writing a new spread if you close the position within the first 2 calendar days of putting it on. Looking at the empirical data, notice there is in fact a sweet spot at 10 days remaining to expiry, and this will be the rule we will follow for the remainder of the book:

> *If we are stopped out during the first 4 days of our trade, then we will roll down and out.*

There are two notable patterns in Figure 4.5. The first is that it always appears better to roll after you are stopped out. While this is potentially counterintuitive—since one might think that it's best to step out of the way of this trade for a bit while it's not working—the data says otherwise. Why might this be? As you recall from Chapter 3, one of the key drivers of the extrinsic value of these OTM options is the implied volatility (IV). It turns out that after a 4% move against you, IV is typically elevated, increasing the premium one receives from selling these options. The average IV of options we sell during our 2013–2023 test window is around 20%, while the average IV of the options we sell after a stop loss has been hit is around 45%! This is why, despite only being stopped out around 10% of the time, we see an increase in mean P&L of more than 10% across the board in Figure 4.5.

Figure 4.5   Reselling at Different Times to Next Sell: Effect on Core SPY 2W 90–96 Put Spread Strategy with ATM Stop Loss; January 1, 2013 – August 31, 2023

	4D	6D	8D	10D	12D	No Roll
Mean P&L (bps)	1.91	1.90	2.00	2.10	1.87	1.68
P&L Volatility (bps)	8.57	8.57	8.39	8.09	8.05	7.89
Mean P&L (bps) / P&L Volatility (bps)	0.22	0.22	0.24	0.26	0.23	0.21
Mean Loss (bps)	-16.75	-16.80	-16.27	-15.78	-16.00	-17.04
Win Rate (%)	88.00	88.00	88.29	88.60	88.07	88.85

ADULT SWIM: OPTION PRICES AND IMPLIED VOLATILITY

We just reviewed the impact of higher IV on our strategy. But let's try to build some additional intuition around this. Figure 4.6 shows the value of a put option at three different implied volatilities (15%, 30%, and 45%). As a proxy for the IV values just discussed, where we saw IV pop from an average of 20% to 45%, let's study the pricing of puts at 15% and 45%. The key thing to notice is that changes in IV are much more

Figure 4.6   Option Price as a Function of IV

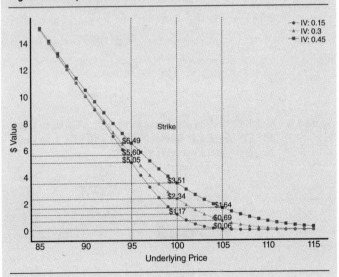

impactful on price when the options are OTM. For example, we see a 5% OTM put option go from $0.06 to $1.64 when IV triples, a 2,700% change, but a 5% ITM put only jumps about 20%.

We also see another pattern in Figure 4.5: it's optimal to roll if the stop loss didn't kick in too fast or too slow. The other force at work here is that equity markets tend to demonstrate strong mean reversion after significant 5-day moves. This means that if the equity market dropped substantially over a 5-day period, we expect the next week or two to be flat to positive, not negative. This is why we see a peak in P&L in the 10D column, since it is close to this 5-day mean reversion period.

Any moves significantly slower or faster than 5 days will not benefit from this mean reversion effect. Nevertheless, it's still beneficial to roll in these cases because you are being more than compensated for the extra risk to the downside via the elevated IV, so one can still implement a stop loss with re-entry here if one chooses to. But in our experience, sticking to the 4-day rule manages both the mental costs and the position P&L.

We have concluded studying how to optimally manage our core SPY trade. It is now time to expand to writing spreads in other markets. This will help us build a diversified portfolio, each spread with distinct risks, further enhancing our strategy's risk-adjusted performance.

Chapter Five

Building a Portfolio

~

To this point, we have focused on an option writing strategy that focuses on a single trade, the 2-week 90–96 SPY put spread with an ATM stop loss. In this chapter, we will expand the analysis to other underlying assets, and consider selling call spreads as well. By trading a broader suite of options, we are able to create a more robust trading strategy with lower risk and potentially higher returns.

Key Takeaways:

1. By diversifying our option writing strategy across a portfolio of different spreads, we lower the probability of maximum loss for the portfolio.

2. Because option premia fluctuate dramatically over time, we should have a wide choice of spreads we can use to improve our odds of generating consistent income.

3. SPY put spreads have more than double the average P&L of similar spreads on TLT and GLD, hence its elevated position as our core trade.

4. A "commonsense" portfolio that diversifies our core SPY trade into other spreads with a low likelihood of simultaneous max loss is our bread-and-butter portfolio solution.

5. More nuanced optimized portfolios can be created, but for most investors, we favor using these as intuition builders rather than live portfolios, given their complexity and generally lower returns.

6. Each trader will have their own unique risk tolerance. Once a trader has identified their most important risk metric, they can scale portfolio positions to the maximum risk levels they are comfortable with.

Motivation

The core SPY trade we have presented thus far is attractive and simple, so why do we need to expand beyond this one trade? A couple of key reasons makes trading a broader basket of spreads a great idea, so let's review those now.

First, we want to expand our option writing choices to minimize our potential max loss. Remember, in our current 2-week 90–96 SPY put spread strategy with ATM stop loss, we are risking 200bps (100bps per week) at any one time. Unfortunately, because both trades rely on the same underlying, our risk of loss is only reduced by differences in our point of entry (which affects strike price and implied volatility). But if we could split the portfolio into two different underliers, we can reduce that instantaneous max risk from 200bps to something less.

This obviously requires that the two trades don't jump to max loss at the same time, a critical assumption on correlation we will dig into in this chapter. The ideal scenario is that the two trades are anti-correlated—if this is true, the potential loss can be reduced to just 100bps! It also requires us to find trades with similar returns to our SPY trade, an empirical question we will also discuss shortly.

For many, 200bps of max loss is likely not very stress-inducing, but most traders will want to lever this up **five to**

ten times to hit a return target, and you are then risking 10–20% at any one time. At the end of this chapter, we will cover the topic of scaling up risk to meet return targets.

The second critical reason to go beyond SPY is that the premium we take in for writing any specific spread will ebb and flow in time. Figure 5.1 shows the premium we take in selling the 2-week 90–96 SPY put spread every week during our lookback period. While the long-term average is an attractive 0.05%, the premium can fluctuate significantly.

Figure 5.1   Premium Taken in Each Week Selling 2W SPY 90–96 Put Spreads with 100bps of Risk; January 1, 2013 – August 31, 2023

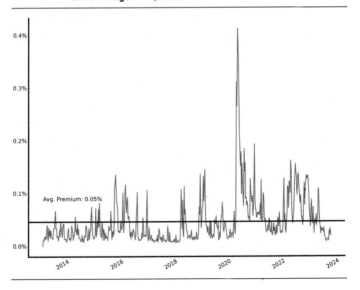

When that premium is low, we will not want to sell the spread if we don't have to, as the return-to-risk is not in our favor (i.e., we aren't being paid enough for the risk we are taking). For example, taking in 10bps while risking 100bps is very attractive, but taking in 1bps for risking 100bps is less likely to deliver strong outcomes.

Hence one needs to have a whole suite of spreads that they can potentially sell to be able to consistently source compelling option-writing opportunities. In Chapter 6 we will discuss a process for monitoring the premia taken in across underliers and sides, and how to implement portfolios that are constantly evolving with the opportunities in the market. For the remainder of this chapter, we focus on the more strategic benefits of adding trades, to minimize downside risks.

Expanding Our Universe

We will now expand our trading universe with four more trades: put and call spreads on TLT (the iShares 20+ Year Treasury Bond ETF) and GLD (the SPDR Gold Shares ETF). One can consider many other underliers, but it's helpful to keep it simple for now as we discuss portfolio construction, a topic that can get very complicated quickly. In Chapter 6, we will present a real-time trade screening process that will easily let you expand to spreads on additional underliers.

Figure 5.2 shows the return profiles of these four new option-writing strategies, still risking 100bps/week on a 2-week option (200bps max loss at any given moment), where we have chosen strikes with a similar risk profile to our core SPY trade, and we have not implemented any risk management tools such as stop losses. By matching risk profiles (volatility and win rate), we allow the user to extend our ATM stop-loss system without any hiccups, as the precise choice of using an ATM stop loss relies heavily on the probability of hitting our sold strike being neither too high nor too low. Remember, we don't want to stop out consistently too early or too late, or we reduce the attractiveness of our strategy.

The most glaring result from Figure 5.2 is that the mean P&L is by far the highest for our original SPY trade, a key reason we have promoted that trade as the core to our ultimate strategy (in addition to a liquidity profile head and shoulders above the rest).

Figure 5.2 Risk/Return Statistics for Different Spread Writing Strategies with Similar Risk Profiles; January 1, 2013 – August 31, 2023

	2W 90–96 SPY Put Spread	2W 109–105 GLD Call Spread	2W 91–95 GLD Put Spread	2W 108–104 TLT Call Spread	2W 93–96 TLT Put Spread
Mean P&L (bps)	1.81	0.92	0.87	0.70	0.93
P&L Volatility (bps)	14.05	10.11	10.31	14.03	15.06
Mean P&L (bps) / P&L Volatility (bps)	0.13	0.09	0.08	0.05	0.06
Mean Loss (bps)	−44.65	−34.14	−35.51	−41.01	−41.38
Win Rate (%)	94.70	95.63	95.93	93.98	93.46

It also clarifies why long-term return enhancement was not a reason mentioned earlier for expanding our trade universe, as the returns for all the other trades are empirically below the return of our core SPY trade. The key strategic benefit from this group of highly liquid trading strategies is to help diversify portfolios and minimize potential loss.

Before we analyze the portfolios of these five trades, we know there is an elephant in the room, so let's address it: Why didn't we add SPY calls to our new roster of potential trades? Figure 5.3 shows the five-matrix strike selection figure for SPY calls, the same framework we used in Chapter 3 to pick our SPY strikes, and the tool used to find the risk-matching strikes for TLT and GLD shown in Figure 5.2. You will immediately notice in Panel A that selling call spreads is, on average, a losing proposition. There are two key reasons for this.

First, remember you are selling a call spread. You are selling protection against a small gain (the lower strike) while buying back protection against a huge gain (the higher strike). For all the behavioral reasons highlighted in Chapter 1, there are few sellers of this huge gain potential (the higher strike). In fact, you are competing with them! As a result, the statistics on buying these deep OTM call options are terrible, as identified in Chapter 1. Secondly, by selling the near-the-money call option, we expose ourselves to the drift higher in equity markets, the proverbial

Figure 5.3   Selection Framework for Selling SPY Call Spreads (2w);
January 1, 2013 – August 31, 2023

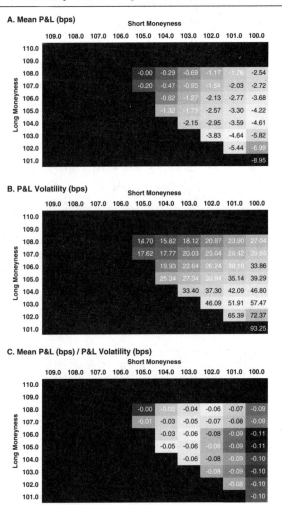

A. Mean P&L (bps)

Short Moneyness

Long Moneyness	109.0	108.0	107.0	106.0	105.0	104.0	103.0	102.0	101.0	100.0
110.0										
109.0										
108.0					-0.00	-0.29	-0.69	-1.17	-1.76	-2.54
107.0					-0.20	-0.47	-0.93	-1.54	-2.03	-2.72
106.0						-0.62	-1.27	-2.13	-2.77	-3.68
105.0						-1.32	-1.73	-2.57	-3.30	-4.22
104.0							-2.15	-2.95	-3.59	-4.61
103.0								-3.83	-4.64	-5.82
102.0									-5.44	-6.99
101.0										-8.95

B. P&L Volatility (bps)

Short Moneyness

Long Moneyness	109.0	108.0	107.0	106.0	105.0	104.0	103.0	102.0	101.0	100.0
110.0										
109.0										
108.0					14.70	15.82	18.12	20.87	23.90	27.04
107.0					17.62	17.77	20.03	23.04	26.42	29.85
106.0						19.93	22.64	26.24	30.10	33.86
105.0						25.34	27.34	30.94	35.14	39.29
104.0							33.40	37.30	42.09	46.80
103.0								46.09	51.91	57.47
102.0									65.39	72.37
101.0										93.25

C. Mean P&L (bps) / P&L Volatility (bps)

Short Moneyness

Long Moneyness	109.0	108.0	107.0	106.0	105.0	104.0	103.0	102.0	101.0	100.0
110.0										
109.0										
108.0					-0.00	-0.02	-0.04	-0.06	-0.07	-0.09
107.0					-0.01	-0.03	-0.05	-0.07	-0.08	-0.09
106.0						-0.03	-0.06	-0.08	-0.09	-0.11
105.0						-0.05	-0.06	-0.08	-0.09	-0.11
104.0							-0.06	-0.08	-0.09	-0.10
103.0								-0.08	-0.09	-0.10
102.0									-0.08	-0.10
101.0										-0.10

Figure 5.3 (Continued)

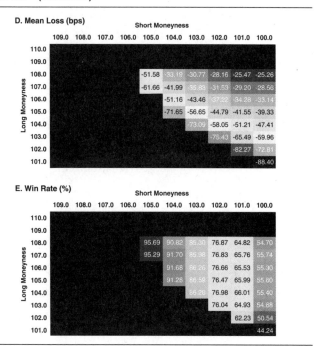

D. Mean Loss (bps)

Short Moneyness

Long Moneyness	109.0	108.0	107.0	106.0	105.0	104.0	103.0	102.0	101.0	100.0
110.0										
109.0										
108.0					-51.58	-33.19	-30.77	-28.16	-25.47	-25.26
107.0					-61.66	-41.99	-35.83	-31.53	-29.20	-28.56
106.0						-51.16	-43.46	-37.22	-34.28	-33.14
105.0						-71.65	-56.65	-44.79	-41.55	-39.33
104.0							-73.09	-58.05	-51.21	-47.41
103.0								-75.43	-65.49	-59.96
102.0									-82.27	-72.81
101.0										-88.40

E. Win Rate (%)

Short Moneyness

Long Moneyness	109.0	108.0	107.0	106.0	105.0	104.0	103.0	102.0	101.0	100.0
110.0										
109.0										
108.0					95.69	90.82	85.30	76.87	64.82	54.70
107.0					95.29	91.70	85.98	76.83	65.76	55.74
106.0						91.68	86.26	76.66	65.53	55.30
105.0						91.28	86.58	76.47	65.99	55.80
104.0							86.28	76.98	66.01	55.40
103.0								76.04	64.93	54.68
102.0									62.23	50.54
101.0										44.24

"stocks for the long run." Particularly over the past few decades, we have seen an increasing propensity for the market to outperform expectations for these near-the-money strikes. Whether this is a cyclical phenomenon, or tied to broader issues around changing market structure, is a subject of fierce debate among market practitioners and academics. Regardless, it's a debate we can opt out of by skipping the call spreads.

ADULT SWIM: IMPLIED VS. REALIZED VOLATILITY

In Chapter 3 we discussed the broad option ecosystem and encouraged a bias toward the selling of options when there is an extra premium baked into them due to behavioral biases of the buyers. In nerd option world this is analyzed by comparing implied volatility with realized volatility. If implied volatility is higher than realized volatility, then there is indeed a behavioral bias premium created by option buyers.

To assess volatility, we plot the distribution of returns realized in SPY versus the frequency of returns that are expected from the implied volatility. Figure 5.4 plots the realized frequency of SPY returns as bars and overlays on top of the expected frequency of returns from the implied volatility (Marshall, Prakash, J, and Medarametla, 2023). As you can see, to the left of ATM, where we are selling puts, there are many return levels where the realized number of returns are less than what is "baked" into the implied volatility of the option market. These points show up as visible white space between the line graph and the bars.

On the flipside, when we consider return events that are positive, we do not see many instances where

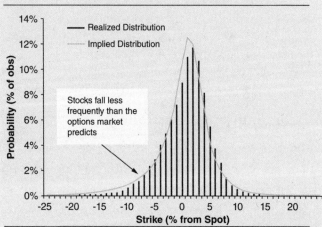

Figure 5.4   SPY Implied vs. Realized Volatility, 1996–2023

the implied distribution is above the realized distribution. In fact, we see the opposite: call IV is often too low versus what is realized, pointing out that buying rather than selling calls would be the smart money move.

It's very important to recognize that the difference between implied and realized only matters when considered in the context of many, many trades. An implied volatility above realized volatility can be thought of as the house "edge" for a casino (or insurance company). But this does not mean we will win every bet if realized volatility is below implied volatility, just as a casino will not win every bet.

> This is how quantitative strategists find these biases; we don't survey people and measure their irrationality. We are simply looking at implied versus realized volatilities.

A "Commonsense" Portfolio

We are now ready to build our first portfolio. As mentioned earlier, our core motivation for incorporating additional trades to our portfolio is to lower our max loss at any one moment in time. Instead of just running an SPY strategy, which had the most attractive risk-adjusted return of the group, we can now run a smaller position in SPY alongside a few other positions to still earn similar returns but with substantially lower max loss. This is a simple example of building a diversified portfolio, focused on diversifying max loss. Portfolio diversification should consider other risk metrics as well (for example, volatility), but for now let's focus on the single metric of drawdown.

The main step in pulling this off is to figure out which trades will not lose big when our core SPY trade has a significant loss. To address this requirement, we first need to agree on what we mean by a "big loss." Since our SPY trade buys back the tail 10% OTM, we're generally thinking about situations where SPY would lose 10% or more over 1–2 weeks, and we would experience the max possible loss on our capped risk spread.

Intuitively this only happens during major risk-off events such as the 2020 global pandemic. In these events we would expect both gold (GLD) and Treasury bonds (TLT) to rally on a flight to safety. The role of these two assets as "safety" trades suggests that a portfolio that writes GLD puts and TLT puts, alongside our core SPY trade, should avoid simultaneous max losses in multiple spreads when SPY has a big drawdown, and our SPY spread moves strongly against us.

Let's see if we can confirm this intuition with some data. Figure 5.5 shows the losses on our five trades in every instance where the SPY put spread trade lost money, even if just the tiniest amount. As noted, we are focused on max loss situations for SPY, where the solid bar is near a 100bps loss.

Of our four diversifiers, the "worst" were TLT calls, which rose sharply during COVID, exactly as we would expect during a flight to safety. We also see an outcome that is counter to our original intuition, as gold (GLD) sold off sharply in the later stages of the pandemic. Unfortunately, this result is a byproduct of the use of leverage in portfolios. Remember, one of our roles as an options seller is to provide leverage to market participants. When portfolios experience losses, they will sometimes be forced to withdraw that leverage. As the

Figure 5.5   Spread Losses Every Time SPY Trade Loses - 100bps Max Loss; January 1, 2013 – August 31, 2023

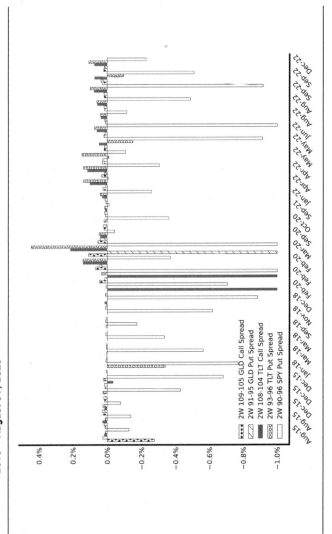

leverage is withdrawn, all assets fall in price. You have likely read about these events in the financial press, along with the phrase "the correlations changed unexpectedly" or "in a crisis, all correlations go to one." Hopefully, now you understand these events a bit better.

Unfortunately, for practical purposes, we must view these outlier events as a "cost of doing business" and simply make sure our risk profile adequately considers the potential for these simultaneous losses. As a result, we will continue to assume that the biggest simultaneous loss risk to a portfolio heavily tilted to SPY puts is on the call side of GLD, while always scaling our portfolio to reflect the low probability risk that our diversification will fail.

Armed with the view that TLT puts and GLD puts shouldn't generally lose alongside our core SPY put spread, the commonsense portfolio we will put forth is 50% SPY put spread, 25% GLD put spread, and 25% TLT put spread. We keep a large position in SPY put spreads given its favorable returns, and then we diversify evenly between GLD and TLT puts, since their return and risk profiles are very similar but have the potential to help minimize simultaneous losses. Whenever you can diversify to more distinct trades with similar return profiles, do it!

Figure 5.6 compares this portfolio to a 100% portfolio of our 2W 90–96 SPY put strategy. Now that we are talking

Figure 5.6   Commonsense Portfolio: 50% 2W 90–96 SPY Put Spread, 25% 2W 94–97 TLT Put Spread, 25% GLD 2W 91–95 Put Spread Strategy; January 1, 2013 – August 31, 2023

	2W 90–96 SPY Put Spread	Commonsense Portfolio
Annualized Return	0.94%	0.67%
Annualized Volatility	1.48%	0.88%
Ann. Return / Ann. Volatility	0.64	0.76
Maximum Drawdown	3.79%	2.03%
Ann. Return / Max Drawdown	0.25	0.33

about portfolios, we are going to start using statistics more common to studying complete strategies rather than single trades. We are now annualizing statistics like return and volatility. We have also introduced maximum drawdown, which is the largest peak-to-trough move from highwater mark during the entire backtest period.

We see that we have cut the maximum drawdown by almost 50% while only reducing return by about 30%. While not as extreme as our hopes of cutting risk without any impact on returns (a caricatured description to get the point across), this is a realistic and welcome amount of reduction in return for the reduction we get in maximum drawdown.

Also, note that the volatility is down about 40%. The combination of returns down 30% and volatility down 40% leads to a risk-adjusted return ratio that increases from 0.64 to 0.76, a very nice win. So, from two distinct lenses of risk, we have enhanced our risk-adjusted returns with the simple risk management notion of avoiding simultaneous max loss.

Optimized Portfolios

The portfolio construction proposal thus far was a simple one, based on the most obvious of downside risk management concepts: avoiding an unnecessarily large max possible loss at an extreme moment in time. But optimizing a portfolio can be much more sophisticated than that.

Figure 5.7 shows our commonsense portfolio next to two portfolios that have been generated by optimization algorithms. The first one generates a portfolio that maximizes the ratio of return to volatility. As you can see, this ratio spikes up from 0.76 to 0.95, at the expense of lower returns, similar to the pattern we observed when we moved from a pure SPY strategy to our commonsense portfolio (Figure 5.6).

So how did the optimizer achieve the higher return/volatility? Look at the portfolio weights in the lower half of Figure 5.7. The optimizer latches on to two facts. First, after SPY the next best return/volatility statistics to turn to for maximizing that number are the GLD trades (see Figure 5.2). Second, since the GLD calls and puts, by definition, will be moving out of sync with one another, there is a strong benefit to pairing these together to minimize volatility. The

Figure 5.7 Commonsense Portfolio Compared to Portfolios with Maximized Return/Volatility and Return/Maximum Drawdown; January 1, 2013 – August 31, 2023

	Commonsense Portfolio	Maximum (Return/Volatility)	Maximum (Return/Max Drawdown)
Annualized Return	0.67%	0.53%	0.46%
Annualized Volatility	0.88%	0.56%	0.61%
Ann. Return / Ann. Volatility	0.76	0.95	0.75
Maximum Drawdown	2.03%	1.07%	0.68%
Ann. Return / Max Drawdown	0.33	0.50	0.67
2W 90–96 SPY Put Spread	50.00%	23.17%	9.16%
2W 109–105 GLD Call Spread	0.00%	34.81%	35.36%
2W 91–95 GLD Put Spread	25.00%	31.17%	26.96%
2W 108–104 TLT Call Spread	0.00%	1.26%	0.00%
2W 93–96 TLT Put Spread	25.00%	9.59%	28.53%

optimizer has identified that selling *both* put and call spreads on GLD is the best trade. And you can clearly observe the effect of these two combined features through the fact that the risk is dominated in GLD (rather than TLT), and then split evenly into calls and puts.

Once again, intuition helps explain these results. Like meme stocks, gold is an asset that inspires fervent devotion (or revulsion) from its fans. The demand for leverage in both directions and protection to the downside is high in GLD, much like equities. Also note that the optimizer eliminates the selling of call spreads on bonds (TLT), lowering it to 1.26% in the return/volatility solution and 0% in the maximum drawdown solution. We see the optimizer intuitively identifying the "flight to safety" embedded in risk-free bonds.

Now let's turn to the maximization of return/drawdown. Once again, the algorithm locks onto the GLD call/put paradigm, but now it also finds the strategy with the highest drawdown contribution (SPY) and moves weight into the lowest drawdown contributor with the best possible return (TLT puts). TLT puts and calls have similar drawdowns, but the puts nicely outperform the calls, *and* they offer the flight to safety benefit, so they are favored. Again, we see returns compromised to reduce the drawdowns from our original SPY-only strategy by more than 80%. Yes, the return in that process has been cut by 50%, but the risk-to-max drawdown ratio has climbed from 0.25 to 0.67!

ADULT SWIM: EFFICIENT FRONTIERS

If you go down the rabbit hole of optimization, you will undoubtedly run into plots like the one shown in Figure 5.8. Here we plot the return and volatility of every possible portfolio one can make using our five core trades. Volatility is of course only one possible measure of risk, and you can just as easily create this plot with any risk metric you like (e.g., max loss, drawdown,

Figure 5.8   Efficient Frontier

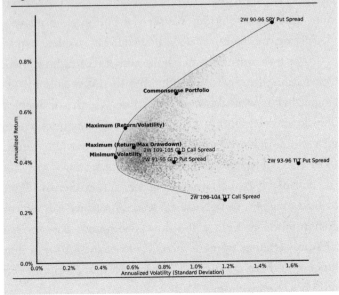

etc.). In this example, we plot volatility as it is the most common risk metric to use in managing portfolios. The line on the plot is known as the "efficient frontier," and it represents the lowest volatility portfolio for every possible level of return. We always want to make sure that our portfolio is somewhere near this line, or else we are being inefficient with our portfolio, since for the same return target we could be running with lower risk. Notice that our commonsense portfolio is tucked nicely next to the efficient frontier, efficient enough from our perspective.

These optimizations give you some great intuition on how you may want to build your own portfolios. The core decision is return versus risk. If you focus on high return trades, you will take on more risk. If you focus on minimizing drawdowns, the extreme opposite of returns, you will lower your returns. But we now need to offer a warning on using optimizations beyond their helpful intuition.

The optimization results in Figure 5.7 used data from the historical period to build the "optimal portfolio" over that *same* period. This is known as an "in-sample" analysis and should immediately be met with skepticism. Of course, if you build an optimal portfolio for a known set of outcomes, you will get phenomenal results. A bit like taking a test with the answer sheet on your desk. The real challenge is to generate impressive "out-of-sample" portfolios, where your portfolio results are measured over a period that comes after the data set used to build the optimal portfolio. When you review the results of an optimized portfolio out-of-sample, they will generally be significantly less impressive than what you saw in-sample. The key ramification here is that you should take the precise allocation numbers with a grain of salt and use them more as a guide to build intuition.

But there is another big issue here: markets are dynamic. Figure 5.9 shows the 1-year rolling correlations between

Figure 5.9   Rolling 1-Year Correlation of SPY to GLD and TLT

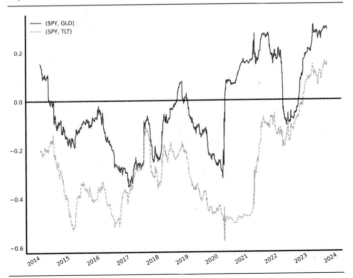

SPY and GLD, as well as SPY and TLT. As you can see, the correlations change dramatically in time. For example, notice the uptick in correlation between TLT and SPY during the rate hike cycle of 2022/2023. If you relied on previous correlation assumptions between these two assets, you would have been selling TLT puts alongside SPY puts, which would have failed you during this "unexpected" period. Using historical data to formalize precise allocations and portfolio risk expectations is very challenging.

Understanding how these tools are used by *other* market participants is often as important as developing the skills to use them on your own. Why? As should be clear by now, many large investors use exactly these techniques in constructing their portfolios. They are all seeing the exact same data as you are, but they may not have the same flexibility that you have to either stop or further diversify your portfolio. The professional investor (e.g., a bond fund manager or large cap equity fund manager) is often at a disadvantage created by their mandate, which prevents them from making these very valuable choices. When you see more market participants "crowding" into a strategy, it can help to raise your awareness of the risks that occur when these crowded positions are unwound.

In our view the best way to create and manage portfolios of spread trades is to assess what's the most important risk to *you* and then use the above concepts as a guidepost.

A portfolio with the objective of buying a house in two years' time is likely far more concerned about drawdown than disappointing returns. On the flipside, a long-term retirement portfolio for a younger investor is likely far more focused on return than risk of drawdown.

Depending on which approach you lean toward, make sure you are adjusting your techniques accordingly as markets evolve. Avoid the risks of "overfitting" your portfolio. In simple terms, if the difference between an optimized portfolio and your intuitive portfolio is minor, stick with your intuition. If there is a major difference, you need to understand why your intuition is failing to capture market behavior. Often, the answer is that the period you are evaluating is too short or contains an unappreciated change in market structure. To us, a commonsense approach that helps reduce the risk of large simultaneous losses, while remaining simple enough to allow an assessment of the impact and risk of changing market regimes, is the best way to go here.

Setting Risk Exposures

So far, we have run all strategies with a max risk of 200bps. This was done to help keep the math simple. But these portfolios are far too risk-averse to meet most investment objectives, as should be clear from Figure 5.6 above. In practice, these strategies are run at higher levels of this max risk, typically in line with other risky assets. For example, a portfolio that is long 100% SPY would expect to have weekly average risk of approximately 200bps, roughly 20× higher than our examples. We can match these portfolios by increasing the sizes of our trades while retaining the benefit of knowing our losses are still capped.

Once you choose how you would like to build your portfolio, from the choices presented in Figure 5.7 or some other method, you have officially established the risk metric that matters to you. Say, for example, you want to focus on avoiding simultaneous max losses and you want to do it in the simple format prescribed in the commonsense portfolio. You are then focused on max loss as your key risk measure, so setting your risk exposure is all about how much max loss you are willing to stomach. In the commonsense portfolio, max loss expectations are around 1%, so if you are comfortable with a max instant loss of 8%, you can scale the strategy up 8×. This would leave you with a return of around 5.3%. Since your strategy doesn't require a cash outlay (remember we are receiving premiums), we also earn on the cash in our account, typically T-Bill yields. Suddenly the attractiveness becomes clearer—5.3% plus T-Bills is currently higher than the historical return on equities, with less risk!

Of course, we haven't layered our ATM stop loss into this discussion yet. Some traders, like the authors, who gravitate toward a max loss portfolio construction mandate, will also consider the benefits of their stop losses here. While our eight-times levered commonsense portfolio had a max loss of 8%, assuming our TLT and GLD puts didn't move in sync with SPY, our expected max loss is much lower due to our ATM stop-loss system. So, the risk exposure you will put on could be more of a hybrid decision process, combining max loss with expected max loss.

Figure 5.10 shows the expected loss of our biweekly SPY spreads, each with 100bps of max risk, as a function of SPY return over a single day. Our ATM stop loss will kick

Figure 5.10 Single-Day Scenario Analysis: Core SPY Trade Positions vs. SPY

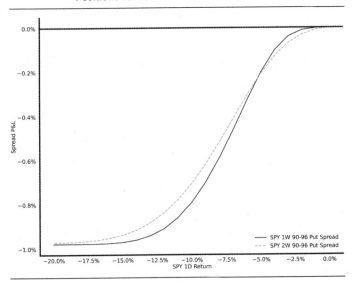

in at 4% down, where the spread expiring in one week is only down 10bps, and the spread expiring in two weeks is down 13bps. So, a max possible loss of 200bps only has an expected max loss of not even 25bps.

The next chapter will take us from theory to practice. One of the key recommendations as you begin to implement this strategy is to take it slow. The most important reason to do this is to find your personal comfort with risk. No one can tell you how *you* should manage risk; it's the ultimate personal question. Start trading the strategy in its simplest form, and as you do so, take note of your own emotional state. The reaction that you have to your gains and losses will help identify your risk profile, so you can figure out what risk management framework is best for you.

Chapter Six

From Theory
to Practice

AT THIS POINT YOU have all the theoretical and empirical knowledge you need to intelligently sell options. It is now time to learn how to implement these concepts in the real world and begin what will hopefully be a fun and lucrative trading journey. In this chapter we will present a real-time trade selection process, review trading best practices, and offer some softer perspectives on how you should approach the first six months trading this strategy.

Key Takeaways:

1. A live option screener will be your key tool for selecting precise spreads to sell in your portfolio. We have created a simple option screener for our readers at www.tradingoptionslikethepros.com.

2. The optimal spreads will be those with the highest expected return that simultaneously satisfy your desired risk profile (defined by win rate and mean loss here).

3. Always use limit orders when trading; never use market orders.

4. Use a trading platform that can scale with you in your journey from novice to professional trader. The platform should also have low commissions and helpful trading tools.

5. Start live trading by selling a single spread contract to get used to your trading tech stack and the process of trading limit orders. Then start trading a single spread in size, to monitor your emotions during the trade, updating strikes, sizing, or risk management techniques to fit your personality.

6. Always be aware of your own behavioral biases as a strategist. Confirmation, recency, and overconfidence biases must be monitored and avoided to run a profitable system consistently.

Option Screener

The first practical step in trading an option writing strategy live is to decide which markets to sell options in. In this book, we have limited the discussion to only three underlying markets, for simplicity's sake. But there is a much wider universe of underliers to consider, and we need a real-time system to be able to find the most interesting trades from that very broad universe. In this section, we describe a simple screening process that accomplishes this. As a service to our readers, we have made the screening tool used in this process available at www.tradingoptionslikethepros.com.

But there is more to a screener than just being able to cast a wide net. Thus far, we have selected trades (underlier, side, and strikes) based on long historical lookbacks. But markets are constantly evolving, and you always need to ensure that today still offers the same opportunity as the history you are familiar with. You could wake up and find that a market you have traded for years now offers such low premia that it is no longer worth selling these spreads. Or you may wake up one day to find that the risk of a market has changed, and you need to update your strikes. Every time you write a new spread, you will want to ensure that the trade you are doing is attractive and aligned with your desired risk profile.

The other key real-world ingredient we haven't discussed yet is the liquidity of a spread. The underliers we have considered in this book so far are all very liquid, easy-to-trade securities. And for the most part their options are quite liquid as well. But when you use a screener to consider any possible market, strike, and expiry, the liquidity can dramatically change, even for the most liquid underliers. Hence, it's paramount in a screening framework to be hyper-focused on liquidity. There are many high-performing strategies out there with incredibly low liquidity, and your goal is to always find maximum returns while ensuring sufficient liquidity for your trade sizes.

Just because we've done the trade before, doesn't mean it's safe to do again. Remember Aesop's fable of the Fox and the Lion:

The Fox & the Lion

A very young Fox, who had never before seen a Lion, happened to meet one in the forest. A single look was enough to send the Fox off at top speed for the nearest hiding place.

The second time the Fox saw the Lion, he stopped behind a tree to look at him a moment before slinking away.

But the third time, the Fox went boldly up to the Lion and, without turning a hair, said, "Hello, there, old top."

Moral: Familiarity breeds contempt. Acquaintance with evil blinds us to its dangers.

Figure 6.1 shows a simple screener on just the three underliers focused on in this book: SPY, GLD, and TLT. We assume each spread risks 100bps and we limit ourselves to the top twenty spreads for presentation purposes, in this case sorted by the first column, Expected Return.[1] We have also filtered out any spreads with a spread width of less than 3%, to trim the universe of tight spreads that we know will have very high mean losses (which we have steered clear of thus far based on our risk preferences).

We use this tool by scanning each row, starting from the top, and look for the first spread for a given underlier that satisfies our risk profile we have settled on for our trading. Say you agree to trade the risk profile set forth throughout this book, which is win rates near 95% and mean losses below 45bps. You choose the row with the highest expected return that matches those criteria for the trailing 1-year period. Columns four and five contain the data on win rate and mean losses, respectively.

For instance, considering SPY puts, the spread with the highest expected return is in row seven. Its 1-year win rate is 98% and it has a mean loss of 14bps over that period. This absolutely satisfies our high win rate/low tail risk criteria, so we can stop here. If you want to get more sophisticated, you

---

[1] Expected Return = win rate * current premium – (1 – win rate) * mean loss.

Figure 6.1   Option Screener, Risking 100bps, Minimum Spread Width of 2%

	Names	Expected Return (bps)	Current Premium (bps)	1 Year Win Rate (%)	1 Year Mean Loss (bps)	Bid-Ask Slippage (%)
1	2W 108.0–105.0 TLT Call Spread	1.94	3.81	94.00	−27.38	3.45
2	2W 110.0–106.0 TLT Call Spread	1.75	2.30	97.96	−24.94	2.04
3	2W 110.0–107.0 TLT Call Spread	1.74	1.87	97.96	−4.55	1.35
4	2W 110.0–105.0 TLT Call Spread	1.69	2.88	93.88	−16.50	2.67
5	2W 109.0–106.0 TLT Call Spread	1.69	2.39	98.00	−32.63	2.04
6	2W 109.0–105.0 TLT Call Spread	1.67	3.09	94.00	−20.58	2.83
7	2W 93.0–96.0 SPY Put Spread	0.51	0.81	98.00	−14.26	0.74
8	2W 92.0–96.0 SPY Put Spread	0.49	0.69	98.00	−9.16	0.64
9	2W 92.0–95.0 GLD Put Spread	0.48	0.59	98.00	−4.68	0.33
10	2W 91.0–96.0 SPY Put Spread	0.48	0.63	98.00	−7.02	0.59
11	2W 92.0–96.0 GLD Put Spread	0.44	0.82	98.00	−18.22	0.63
12	2W 90.0–96.0 SPY Put Spread	0.43	0.55	98.00	−5.66	0.52
13	2W 89.0–96.0 SPY Put Spread	0.41	0.52	98.00	−4.71	0.49
14	2W 93.0–96.0 GLD Put Spread	0.39	0.93	98.00	−25.70	0.67
15	2W 88.0–96.0 SPY Put Spread	0.39	0.48	98.00	−4.04	0.45
16	2W 90.0–95.0 GLD Put Spread	0.38	0.45	97.96	−3.12	0.30
17	2W 87.0–96.0 SPY Put Spread	0.37	0.44	98.00	−3.41	0.42
18	2W 90.0–96.0 GLD Put Spread	0.36	0.63	97.96	−12.74	0.50
19	2W 91.0–95.0 GLD Put Spread	0.36	0.44	98.00	−3.74	0.25
20	2W 91.0–96.0 GLD Put Spread	0.34	0.65	98.00	−14.99	0.50

could keep going down the list and consider whether any spreads making less money are more interesting from a risk perspective. For instance, the next SPY trade is in row eight, where the expected return we take in has dropped by only 0.02bps (from 0.51bps to 0.49bps), while the win rate has stayed the same and the mean loss has dropped down to 9bps from 14bps. In this case we would absolutely sell the spread in row eight over the one in row seven since the expected return has barely changed while the mean loss has gone down significantly.

Now check out row 10. We again see the same pattern of similar expected returns but lower mean losses. The difference between each row is that the spread is getting wider and wider. This is precisely why we favored wider spreads when we chose our core strikes in Chapter 3: the risk of quickly blowing through the full spread is lower, minimizing the mean loss.

An important question at this stage is: "What is a sufficient expected return to enter a trade?" Is the 50bps just discussed for SPY put spreads interesting enough to trade? There are several things to consider here. Figure 5.2 is a great place to start answering this question. If the expected returns calculated in Figure 6.1 are significantly less than the longer-term expectations of Figure 5.2, you should consider not trading here. The answer also depends on what other opportunities there are. If there are no other significantly more attractive opportunities in the broader market, then you might have to be more open to an asset where the current return expectations are below your historically driven expectations. Unfortunately, the much-maligned statement of Charles Prince, interim CEO of Citibank ahead of the 2007 mortgage crisis, remains true for most investors: "As long as the music is playing, you've got to get up and dance."

Finally, we will point out that screening can indeed be significantly more complex. In our work at Simplify Asset Management, we utilize about 20 more filters in our screening tool. We consider things like the trailing five days of performance, to ensure we are not entering a trade that can seriously mean revert against us (building on the mean reversion effect discussed in Chapter 4). We also consider shorter lookbacks for our expected returns (and all the underlying statistics) to provide even more granular perspectives on how each market is evolving. As you build sophistication, you will certainly want to consider more advanced screening parameters for yourself.

Trading

Now that we have decided which spreads we would like to sell in our portfolio this week, we are ready to trade. In our professional capacity, we trade with many different brokers, but one excellent one we use, also accessible to retail traders, is Interactive Brokers (IB). We will be presenting the trading workflow using images from IB's trading platform "Trader Workstation." There are plenty of other good places to trade options, but one key thing that stands out about IB that we want readers to consider, is the ability to scale with you from beginning trader to consummate professional. There aren't many other brokers out there servicing both the smallest retail traders and the largest investment managers. Regardless of the precise broker you use, the workflow for trading options is universal, so the process we now present can be applied to any trading platform.

To sell a spread in IB, you will first open the "Order Entry" screen. Here, you will work through eight steps, labeled 1–8 in Figure 6.2. Let's walk through each step now.

1. **Contract.** This is where we specify the precise spread we want to sell: underlier, strikes, expiry. We've consistently phrased our option strikes in moneyness terms,

Figure 6.2   Order Entry

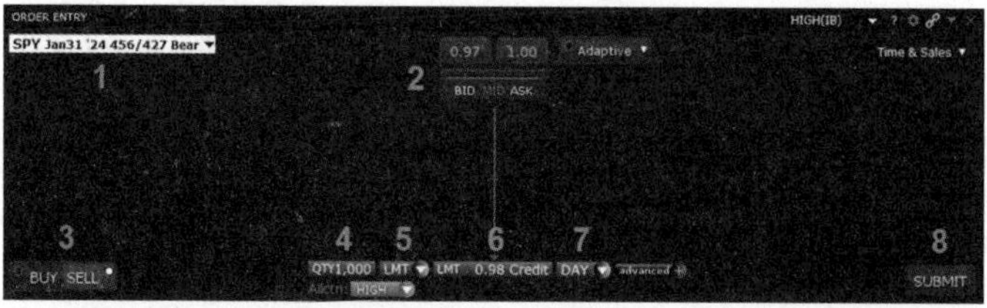

but to convert the conversation into executable trades you will have to convert moneyness to actual strike price. For example, if you are looking to sell a 95 moneyness option on SPY currently trading at $500, the strike is 0.95 * $500 = $475.

2. **Price.** This gives the current pricing of the spread. It shows us the "**bid**," the highest price someone is currently willing to buy the spread at, and the "**ask**," the lowest price someone is willing to sell the spread at. We will always try to execute at the "**mid**," or the midpoint between the bid and the ask. More on this shortly.

3. **Side.** Here we specify that we are selling the spread, not buying it.

4. **Quantity.** This is where you specify how many options contracts you want to sell. Options have a multiplier (typically 1 contract represents 100 shares of the underlying security), which means that if an option price is $1 and you sell one contract, you are bringing in $100, not $1. A classic rookie mistake here is to sell 100 option contracts when you really mean to sell 1. This kind of mistake is very noticeable in the order confirmation window, where you would bring in $10,000 instead of $100. We will review that stage of the trading process shortly.

5. **Order Type.** There are many types of orders traders use. The two most common order types are market and limit orders. Your **market order** will be filled at whatever price is available, with no control over what that might be. For example, if you buy a single contract with a **market order**, it will likely be filled at the ask. But this could be far from mid if the bid–ask spread is wide. Or if you are looking to fill a large quantity, the ask you see might not have enough contracts behind it, and then you will be partially filled before going to the next offer out there, and so on. You don't know where your ultimate fill price will end up.

   This is why we always use **limit orders**, where a specified price, known as the **limit price**, is the max (min) level we are willing to buy (sell) at. We recommend setting this at the mid and letting the market come to you. This way, you are in full control of your fill price, with no possible surprises. Remember, you're the insurance company now, and you have the luxury of being selective with the risks you want to take. More on this to come shortly.

6. **Limit Price.** This is where we set the limit price for our order.

7. **Time in Force.** Orders can be sent to the market to be good for just today (DAY) or until the trader

cancels it, known as Good Til Canceled (GTC). We recommend using DAY to make sure the order isn't mistakenly left open overnight, where a big market move could have you fill your limit order at a price that is no longer attractive to you.

8. **Submit.** This is the button you push when you have fully specified your trade. You will typically get to view an order confirmation page after you push this button, giving you one more look at the trade before transmitting it to the market.

Figure 6.3 shows IB's order confirmation page. You will notice that the precise options you are looking to trade, the quantities, the order type, the limit price, and the time in force are all listed for verification. You also see how much premium you will be receiving, next to "Amount." This is the best place to ensure you didn't make any 100× mistakes by forgetting about the multiplier. This is also a great time to confirm that your limit price is correctly set relative to the most recent bid and ask levels, shown at the top of the window. You will notice that during the few seconds it took for us to go from order entry in Figure 6.2 to confirmation window in Figure 6.3, the bid–ask has slightly moved in our favor. Since the bid is up 1 cent, we could try moving our limit price up to $0.99 instead of the original $0.98, if we are willing to be patient and let the market come to us. Else if we are just

Figure 6.3   Order Confirmation

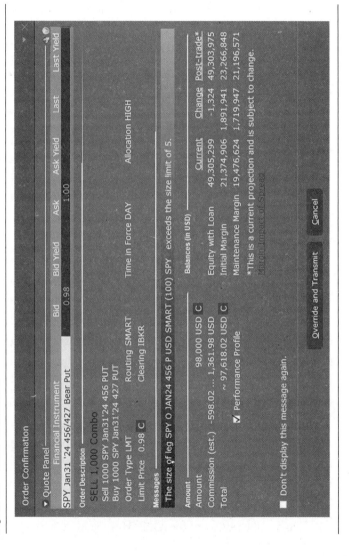

motivated to get the trade done, we could just leave our limit price at the original $0.98.

There is another key piece of information shown in Figure 6.3—the margin you will need for the trades. Any time a trader is selling something they don't own, or if they want to buy more than they have cash for, they need a margin account. The key thing for option writers is knowing whether your margin requirement exceeds the cash in the account. If it does, you will be charged interest on that overage, as it's considered a loan from the broker. In a standard "Reg T" account, for trades held overnight, your portfolio margin is allowed to go up to 2× the cash deposited.

As you can see in Figure 6.3, there are two distinct types of margin. **Initial margin** is the amount needed in your account the first day you put the trade on, while **maintenance margin** is the amount needed in your account after the trade is complete. If you are focused on avoiding consistent interest charges, you will focus on maintaining a margin that stays below your cash deposits. If you want to know whether or not you can get a trade on given your cash and available margin, you will be focused on whether your account still has room for the initial margin of the new trade.

The portfolio shown here has just over $49M of cash in it (which is not transparent from Figure 6.3, since they only report the combined metric of Equity with Loan, so you will just have to take our word for it). In this example, the trade being submitted requires \$1.9M of initial margin, leaving us with plenty of room to execute the current trade and subsequent trades. And from a maintenance margin perspective we still have ample room to do more trades afterward without incurring any interest expenses (there is \$49.3M – \$21.2M = \$28.1M of cash available for margin post-trade).

One nice thing about selling capped risk spread is that the margin needed for a trade is typically about half of the max possible loss from the trade. So, in this case, we sold 1,000 contracts of a spread that could lose \$29 (\$456 – \$427), making our max loss 1,000 * 100 * \$29 = \$2.9M. You see that IB is only asking for about 60% of that amount in maintenance margin (\$1.7M / \$2.9M). Given this low margin requirement, we have found that you can generate attractive returns without ever accessing margin beyond your cash, completely avoiding any interest charges.

You may have noticed in Figure 6.3 that there was a small box checked off, called "Performance Profile." This will open a new window, as shown in Figure 6.4. This is another dialogue that can help us ensure that the trade is being submitted as intended. Here we can confirm again that our strikes are set correctly and the potential payoff is as expected (in the particular case of Figure 6.4, the price axis ends at \$430, so you actually can't see the complete capped-risk payoff). We can also check whether our trade sizing is reasonable by checking data points such as "Max Loss."

Figure 6.4   Payoff Profile

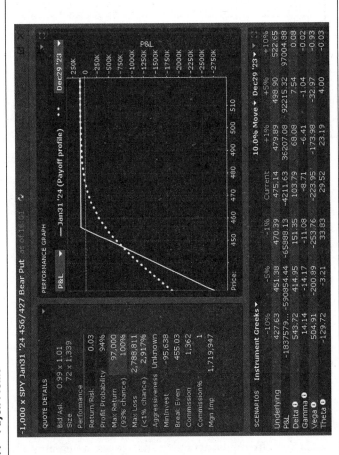

The last IB tool that is worth pointing to is the Market Depth screen, reproduced in Figure 6.5. Remember earlier we mentioned the challenges of market orders with larger order sizes. One can get a lot more sophisticated on this topic if you have access to the market depth. This tool shows you how many contracts are being offered to buy or sell at each price. In Figure 6.5 we have boxes around the highest bid and the lowest ask. These are the bids and asks that are shown earlier in the bid and ask fields in Figures 6.2 and 6.3, but we now see how many contracts are behind each (and the exchange they are sitting on, which isn't too important for us here), at least in "lit markets" that are displayed publicly. By contrast, "dark pools" do not show the prices a buyer or seller is willing to trade at, hence their liquidity is not transparent in market depth charts. We can also now see the price levels that we may need to step down to (as sellers) or up to (as buyers) to fill our full trade size.

Before we leave the discussion on trading, it's important to discuss how the stop loss system discussed in Chapter 4 should be executed. For traders focused on linear instruments (those without a nonlinear, option-like payoff) like equities, futures, and bonds, stop losses are often managed as GTC orders placed immediately after the trade is initially entered. But given the nonlinear nature of options, we cannot rely on standing limit orders in this way. This is because option prices often move in big jumps due to their nonlinearity, potentially

Figure 6.5   Market Depth

Quote Panel

Fnncl Instrmnt	Bid	Ask	Last	Change	Position	Low	High
SPY Jan31 '24 456...	0.98	1.00					

Buttons — Armed

Close Position | Reverse Position | View Account

Deep Book Buttons: AMEX | PSE | MERCURY | ISE | Others

Orders | Log | Trades | Portfolio

Allocation   Action   Quantity   Time in Force   Type   Lmt Price   Aux. Price   Opn ...   Destination   Status

Bid

MM Name	Price	Size	Cum Size	Avg Px	Mn Trd Sz
BOX	0.98	40	40	0.980	
CBOE2	0.98	127	167	0.980	
EMERALD	0.98	40	207	0.980	
PSE	0.98	112	319	0.980	
CBOE	0.97	499	818	0.974	
EDGX	0.97	282	1,100	0.973	
ISE	0.97	604	1,704	0.972	
MERCURY	0.97	149	1,853	0.972	
MIAX	0.97	91	1,944	0.972	

Ask

MM Name	Price	Size	Cum Size	Avg Px	Mn Trd Sz
CBOE2	1.00	118	118	1.000	
PSE	1.00	112	230	1.000	
BOX	1.01	40	270	1.001	
EDGX	1.01	150	420	1.005	
EMERALD	1.01	40	460	1.005	
ISE	1.01	524	984	1.008	
CBOE	1.02	665	1,649	1.013	
MERCURY	1.02	149	1,798	1.013	
MIAX	1.02	91	1,889	1.014	

skipping a precise stop level. Additionally, liquidity can dry up temporarily for options that are moving quickly, which would significantly impact how many contracts get executed within our order. Because of this, the stop loss procedures described in Chapter 4 should be implemented in real time, not as a preset standing order. Once your stop loss price is hit you should then go ahead and execute a limit order to close the trade.

The First Six Months

The first thing you will need to do as a new trader is sign up with a good broker. The broker should be a well-established firm, so you don't have to worry about waking up one day to discover that the firm is shutting down. The broker should also have low commissions (say, less than $1 per contract) and provide interesting trading and analytics tools, like the market depth chart and payoff profiles we reviewed above. And if you are planning on using margin, the firm should charge reasonable borrowing rates. We would recommend IB as a great place to start, as it meets all the criteria just mentioned. Additionally, IB is a platform that can scale with you, from your first single-contract trade to when you are running the biggest hedge fund on Wall Street, as they cater to both the retail crowd as well as some of the largest asset management firms out there.

The next key decision is how much to fund your account with. The key advice here is to fund this account with money you wouldn't miss if it disappeared tomorrow. We say this mainly because we don't want this venture to be stressful to you (or your significant other), and using dollars with real utility in your daily life can lead to serious stress. Second, you don't know if you are going to follow the risk management tools described in this book until you are trading live. There is the risk that your emotions are going to interject in this strategy, which could lead to outcomes that could be catastrophic.

Once your account is funded, the first thing we would recommend doing is putting on a one-contract test trade in any of the spreads that screened well. This simple trade will get you used to the trading workflow and see what trading with limit orders feels like. You may notice that when you use the mid as your limit price, you may not get filled. The closer you push the sell price toward the bid, the higher the chance of it getting filled. So, where you place your order within the bid–ask window is all about how aggressively you want to be in "chasing" the trade. Your process around entering and managing limit orders as the market is moving will become a core competency in this endeavor, so flesh it out with single-contract spreads first.

Once this position is closed, you can take some time to assess the realized P&L, ensuring you understand everything your broker reports to you, including all commissions and any interest charged on your margin (which should be 0 for a trade this size).

Now that the pipes are cleared and we've got our core trading process down, it's time to put on another single-spread trade, this time larger in size. This stage in your journey aims to monitor your emotions during the trade. You might absolutely love the systematic approach outlined in this book, but emotions can take over when there are real dollars at risk. You might find that ATM stop losses are too loose for you, and you are stressing well before the underlying gets to your sold strike. Or you may find that the risk–reward of the strikes we have chosen is too skewed for your liking (e.g., bringing in only a few bps while risking 100bps doesn't feel right). You might even find that selling capped-risk options in any configuration isn't a good match for your personality, which is not uncommon. This is the most nuanced and defining stage of your journey. Here, you may want to reread the core trading chapters of this book and consider other potential strike combinations or risk management techniques to customize the strategy to your personalized preferences. Once you are through this stage of the journey, you are ready to write across a number of underliers and begin building your diversified portfolio.

Beware Assignment

As noted in Chapter 2, ETF options are "American," which means they can be exercised any time before expiry. Hence there is a chance that if we sell an option that becomes ITM, the buyer of the call/put option could exercise their right to buy/sell the security from/to us early, and we as the seller would be "assigned" the option.

As an example, let's say we sold a call option, the stock rises significantly, and we're assigned early. We would then be obliged to sell the corresponding number of shares to the call buyer at the strike price. Unfortunately, in the strategy laid out in this book, we do not already hold the stock to sell. We would have to go buy it before we could deliver it. Since we generally sell more options than we could cover if we were buying the equivalent number of shares represented by our options, we most likely don't have enough cash to go buy the stock in the market.

Let's put this simply—you do not want this to occur. In this scenario, your broker would likely liquidate your portfolio with no advance warning. Once they see you don't have enough margin to cover the necessary share purchases, they will move to protect themselves. Fortunately, the liquidation isn't the end of the world, but you are no longer the one doing the trading in your account. And the broker typically has the right to liquidate holdings beyond those connected to assignment, potentially resulting in multiple positions being closed at prices you don't control.

Thankfully, avoiding this is simple: don't hold short option positions past the ATM stop loss point! You have zero risk of being assigned an option if it is OTM, so before a sold call or put becomes ITM, you will want to close the position as discussed in Chapter 4. Once again, this will be seamless if you follow any stop loss system reviewed in Chapter 4 that closes your position at prices where your option is not yet in-the-money.

Behavioral Biases of Sellers

We've pushed readers of this book to sell options due to a couple of key behavioral biases that make this the profitable side of the trade. But there are biases we need to be cognizant of on this side of the table, too. As strategists, we can succumb to a distinct set of biases that we must consistently ward off. Let's review a few of those now.

Confirmation Bias

After a string of successful bets, we should consider confirmation bias. With growing confidence in our approach, we might unconsciously seek out information or interpret market data to confirm our existing beliefs or strategies, ignoring contradictory evidence suggesting we should be reducing our bets or that we just got lucky for a few spins of the wheel. We always recommend a balanced information gathering and analysis approach to address this risk. Consulting a variety of sources and viewpoints and stressing the importance of being open to adjusting strategies in response to new data is critical.

Anchoring/Recency Bias

The flipside of confirmation bias is anchoring and recency biases, which occur when sellers rely too heavily on either the first piece of information they encounter (such as the P&L on the first trade) or the latest piece of information (such as the P&L on the latest trade) when making decisions about future trades. The critical risk in volatility selling strategies is akin to the market mantra, "Time in the market beats timing the market." In other words, selling options is a slow path to success. We should be fine if we are honoring our risk management rules, based on objective criteria rather than recent results. At the same time, we emphasize the importance of continuously updating analysis with the latest market data. It is always possible that something substantive has changed. And when in doubt, reduce bet sizes; don't abandon strategies.

Overconfidence Bias

Finally, the overconfidence bias occurs when sellers overestimate their ability to predict market movements or the effectiveness of their strategies. Overconfidence can lead to taking on excessive risk or neglecting the need for diversification. The most critical tool in addressing this risk is simply awareness. We encourage backtesting and using historical data but emphasize that the phrase "past performance is not indicative of future results" is not just compliance gibberish. We cannot know the future distribution of possible outcomes, and assuming the past is a perfect guide exposes us to unnecessary risk. We stress the importance of consistently using risk management techniques, like using put spreads rather than selling outright puts, and maintaining a diversified portfolio.

Parting Words

The focus of this book has been how to trade options in a manner that offers a high probability of success while limiting investor risk. It is not an exhaustive text that discusses all the possible ways to use options, but hopefully we've highlighted both the opportunity and the many reasons so many are disappointed with their personal experience in trading options.

Options are complex and there are a million ways to use them, making the learning curve very steep, and often too steep to overcome. By singling out foundational option strategies used by professionals, we hope to have empowered readers with a sophisticated starting point in a long and enjoyable journey into option trading.

There is so much more to learn about options than what's in this book. In fact, there is much more one can do with the strategies presented in this manuscript (e.g., sell single stock spreads, use timing mechanisms in your filters, etc). We hope you take advantage of the opportunity to keep learning and refining what we have reviewed in this book to match your own risk tolerances and investment objectives. We wish you the best of luck on this journey and encourage you to reach out to us on social media with questions and feedback.

Bibliography

Buffett. (n.d.). *Billionaire Philosophy*. Retrieved from https://www.youtube.com/watch?v=jtRttatXyVk.

Gonzalez and Wu. (1999). On the Shape of the Probability Weighting Function. *Cognitive Psychology*, 129–166.

Marshall, Prakash, J, and Medarametla. (2023). *New Models for Asymmetric Investing*. Goldman Sachs.

de Silva, So, and Smith. (2023). Losing is Optional: Retail Option Trading and Expected Announcement Volaility. *SSRN*, 1–65.